Shaun McLeod

Chamber

Shaun McLeod

Chamber

Dance Improvisation, Masculine Embodiment,
and Subjectivity

VDM Verlag Dr. Müller

Imprint

Bibliographic information by the German National Library: The German National Library lists this publication at the German National Bibliography; detailed bibliographic information is available on the Internet at http://dnb.d-nb.de.

Any brand names and product names mentioned in this book are subject to trademark, brand or patent protection and are trademarks or registered trademarks of their respective holders. The use of brand names, product names, common names, trade names, product descriptions etc. even without a particular marking in this works is in no way to be construed to mean that such names may be regarded as unrestricted in respect of trademark and brand protection legislation and could thus be used by anyone.

Cover image: www.purestockx.com

Publisher:
VDM Verlag Dr. Müller Aktiengesellschaft & Co. KG , Dudweiler Landstr. 125 a, 66123 Saarbrücken, Germany,
Phone +49 681 9100-698, Fax +49 681 9100-988,
Email: info@vdm-verlag.de

Zugl.: Melbourne, Deakin University, Diss., 2002

Produced in USA and UK by:
Lightning Source Inc., La Vergne, Tennessee, USA
Lightning Source UK Ltd., Milton Keynes, UK
BookSurge LLC, 5341 Dorchester Road, Suite 16, North Charleston, SC 29418, USA

ISBN: 978-3-639-04545-1

Table of Contents

ACKNOWLEDGEMENTS

I would like to acknowledge and thank the following people for their help and support during this project:

Kim Vincs, Annie Duncan, Suzanne Hurley, Cobie Orger, Kath Papas, Matt Delbridge, Mark Lang, Ben Grant, Dianne Reid, Rachelle Roberts, Heather Ruck and Becky Furniss.

David Corbet for the soundscape, and Christina Shepard and Cormac Lally for the video in *Chamber*.

Most of all I owe an enormous debt of gratitude to Simon Ellis, Martin Kwasner and Jacob Lehrer for their contributions, untiring commitment and superb dancing in *Chamber*.

PREFACE

The writing of this book is entwined with the process of making a live dance work. *Chamber* was originally performed in July 2002 at Dancehouse in Melbourne, Australia. *Chamber* was Choreographed and directed by Shaun McLeod and performed by Simon Ellis, Martin Kwasner and Jacob Lehrer. The performance was accompanied by live soundscore by David Corbet and with video by Cormac Lally and Christina Shepard.

The dancing in *Chamber* sits somewhere between set choreography and improvisation. It inhabits the uncomfortable space that is sometimes called 'structured improvisation' and is an engagement with aspects of both camps.

This writing is an alter image of that process and a way of thinking through and articulating the strains that coalesced into the final performance work. This work charts some of the challenges of improvisation and its relationship to choreographic fixity, and of the development of a personal choreographic process.

Enquiries regarding the performance of *Chamber* can be sent to smcleod@deakin.edu.au

INTRODUCTION

Chamber is an examination of the links between dance improvisation, embodiment and masculine subjectivity. The project began as a response to the current difficulties of defining masculine identity. This beginning was a recognition, made possible by feminist explorations of gender identity, that the idea of masculinity has historically been assumed as the norm and therefore unworthy of attention, rendering it 'invisible'. The performance component of *Chamber*, then, is an attempt to stage a small slice of masculinity and the experiences of the three male dancers involved, as a metaphor for 'problematizing' what otherwise is taken for granted.

A key aim of the project is to align men with embodiment. *Chamber* attempts to define the performers' bodily practices in a specific way so as to illuminate alternatives to the authoritative but limited representations of 'hegemonic masculinity'. Indeed, the act of men dancing in and of itself presents a particular challenge to hegemonic masculinity, with men engaging in a 'feminine' form of embodiment.

Beginnings of the project

The original line of questioning in beginning this project was an enquiry as to why so few men pursue dance, or more specifically contemporary dance, as a form of physical expression. Why don't scores of other men dance, when I find it so rewarding and enriching? What is it about contemporary dance or indeed any form of dance which men find difficult to align with their sense of themselves and the construction of their masculinity? In the fixed gender delineation that western societies demand, the association of dancing with femininity has strongly discouraged men from dancing. But if dancing is seen as effeminate, what else might be involved or at stake?

In contemplating these issues it became apparent that men's distrust lay not specifically with dancing but with the way men regard many embodied practices. In particular, the distrust of dancing is bound to a suspicion of any man who uses his body in a way that differs from a strictly limited and tightly defined understanding. The problem, as I saw it, lay not with dancing itself, but with the way men view what constitutes masculinity and with how they see themselves.

As one of the relatively small number of men who want to dance, my experience as a dancer has been primarily in the company of women, as contemporary dance is to a large degree a form that has been carved out and defined by visionary female artists. In a certain way, I think I was completely at ease with this situation and often felt at odds with aspects of masculinity in the stereotypical sense. Dancing was actually a way to circumnavigate the demands of the backslapping fraternity. Male friendship is, I suspect, often a problematic and fraught area. While men obviously spend a great deal of time together, they do so within strongly defined and restrictive boundaries. It is perhaps a cliché to say that men do not talk about their emotions and that they often remain alienated from each other. Communication in a meaningful, open and trusting environment is still something groups of men can find difficult to achieve [Ryan, 1985].

And yet I enjoy the company of men. *Chamber* is a work for male dancers and part of wanting to work with men was simply seeking out the company of like-minded men. I was interested in working with men who are asking the same questions about what constitutes positive communication amongst men. Through this engagement it became apparent that the working questions should not be about why men do *not* dance, but to find the positive perspective on the same issue. In other words what happens when men *do* dance? As a male dancer and choreographer, why do I dance? What is it about dancing that is useful in defining identity for me and the other male dancers on this project? How do men embody these and other issues, and how can these perspectives be realized in choreography?

Men experience questions such as these in many different ways. They are, ultimately, subjective. How a movement feels to a dancer is often different to how it is perceived by an audience. How that movement feels to one dancer as compared to another will also be hard to empirically define. This is the same for both men and women. But male self-definition located through sensing and feeling, and in other ways regarded as marginal to masculinity, remains restricted and problematic. Laurence Goldstein summarizes a trend:

> *If recent writings are any indication, the task of men's studies is to recover from history and from empirically-observed behaviours in the present day, that sense of choice and variety in self-definition that so many women have embraced as a means of personal and social liberation.* [Goldstein, 1994: vii]

Chamber reflects the spirit of this observation. It is a plea for alternative expressions of masculine embodiment by defining the subjective danced experiences of the men involved. But to give definition to the multiplicity of these subjective experiences, particularly when dealing with a body-centred activity, requires a methodology that can embrace the specific needs of dancing itself.

Theoretical perspectives
In my experience, dance has always been an elusive creature to adequately describe. Attempts to identify precise, indisputable meanings inevitably fail as interpretations and relationships between movement and language differ so greatly. The number of responses to a non-representational piece of dancing are inevitably numerous and inextricably bound to the performance. All verbal description is removed from the primary experience, a dilution of the intensity and power of dance in its original immediacy. This is true for both dancer and viewer. Subjectivity seems inevitable, thus rendering dance, in its primary form, resistant to theories which demand absolutes and quantifiable facts.

Contemporary dance in particular has been founded on the premise that the body of work and knowledge has been strengthened by individual choreographers who strive to find a way of moving that departs from what has come before. Attempts to codify techniques and movement vocabularies beyond the life of the individual who created them, seem to stultify and deaden rather than extend. No major choreographer has emerged who has used Martha Graham's technique for example, without significantly or even radically departing from her legacy. Each new generation undoubtedly takes up where their immediate forebears left off in order to make dance relevant to *their* lives.

It is this drive towards subjectivity in dance that has always attracted my attention. Attempts to understand what dancing best means for me, for my body, have been informed by many things. Objective observations of my capabilities (for example, the limited mobility of my hip sockets which in turn limits the range of leg movement) as well as the subjective impressions of others ("you seem like a very fluid, lyrical dancer") have helped define my dancing. The subjectivity of my own experience of how I move or how I feel when I move has been equally important. The differentiation of movement qualities and the sensations accompanying these inevitably lead to choices about what movements are preferable for my body and sensibility.

The way in which I choreograph flows from this knowledge of my own physique, and my aesthetic is interwoven with the sensation of my own movement. As with any dancing it must be executed; it cannot be purely imagined and thus removed from the body. Consequently, attempts to theoretically situate this project must acknowledge that an objective perspective is not singularly sufficient to understand how I choreograph or how I experience dancing. Dance has a very specific history and training that revolves around the needs, experiences and signification of the body. To be a dancer is to work with the sensations and capabilities of the body in a way that cannot be adequately transcribed into language. Dance is always experiential at some level, always subjective, and to do justice to its full range of meanings and interpretations, any theory that engages with it must acknowledge this.

Nevertheless, in researching this project I developed concerns about the ways in which dance practice and dance experiences were often insufficiently addressed by intellectually centred theoretical positions. A strict hierarchy, with an impressive historical lineage, is embedded in the traditional theoretical stance of much of Western thought and philosophy. It is a stance which privileges and glorifies the workings of the mind or consciousness, and which devalues the experiences and the artefacts of the body [Grosz, 1994]. This new issue began to drive my search for an appropriate theoretical framework. This was the desire to find an intellectual context which was not inherently dichotomous; that is to say one which did not separate mind and body and denigrate the physical dimension. The experiences of the body needed to be acknowledged as important, valuable, central and complex, but also to acknowledge that corporeal practices are subjectively experienced. This seemed crucial for me to understand how the specific needs of dance, or at least my participation in it, could be fully articulated.

This is not to suggest that the objective dimension is not equally as important in analysing the manifestations of embodied practices. Nor do I make a claim for dance as an essentialist practice. Dancers' bodies are like any body in the sense that they can be viewed as gender-coded or socially constructed. But in defining a process for *Chamber* itself I have aimed to focus on the subjectively experienced dimension of how movement is created from an internal perspective. This 'looking inside' for the impulse or inspiration to move in no way negates the objectively constituted dimension of the final performance. But it does necessitate an investigation that cites embodied subjectivity, or more specifically, an embodied masculine subjectivity, as being central and valid. The challenge then became to align embodiment and masculine subjectivity within a theoretical context.

One of the key political aims of the feminist movement has been to define and describe the specificities of the female body as a way of illuminating and celebrating the differences ascribed to woman. Within feminism the body has often been a primary site of investigation with the female body being the major difference that has historically led men to claim superiority. Conversely, men have traditionally ignored their own bodies except in their capacity to exert power and dominance [Connell, 1995]. Men have historically claimed association with the superiority of mind over body, and assigned the lower ranking of body to women. Consequently, particular strands of feminism have sought to challenge this binary status quo, critique the superiority of mind over body, and celebrate the artefacts and experiences determined by the female body. Feminist philosopher Elizabeth Grosz has been primarily concerned with undermining the dichotomous status of traditional philosophical tenets which inherently subjugate the position of both woman and body. She has piercingly critiqued, from a feminist perspective, the work of seminal male philosophers and theorists (such as Freud, Lacan and Nietzsche) who have been credited with liberating the status of body from the dominance of mind. At issue is whether these (male) theorists have adequately addressed the intricacies and differences of the female body, whether they offer something important to the feminist cause, and whether their ideas have inherent and unacknowledged masculine biases [Grosz, 1994].

However, Grosz has also outlined the important ways in which these theorists dealt with the body and its relationship to subjectivity. A key figure in grappling with the fraught area of embodied subjectivity has been the phenomenologist Maurice Merleau-Ponty. Merleau-Ponty's most radical assertion was that all subjectivity resides in the body, that the category of mind cannot exist without the body, and that aspects of mind and body are inter-linked in their relationships with the world – no duality need exist between them [Grosz, 1994: 86]. Consequently these ideas, as viewed from the feminist angle of Elizabeth Grosz, have formed the principle theoretical platform for this project. This is not in any sense a phenomenological study, but it does share the phenomenological perspective when asking how dance might express masculine subjectivity. This perspective is sympathetic to *Chamber*; it corresponds with the process required of the dancers and myself, to internally monitor and reflect on our responses to the phenomenon – in this instance, dance.

Improvisation and choreographic practice
The methodology for this project centres on the use of improvisation as a means of exploring ideas, creating material and as a performance medium in its own right. *Chamber* is a 'structured improvisation' in that the order of events has been set, as have, to a large degree, the parameters for the movement. But the movement material itself changes between performances. Within this the dancers are required to create the movement of the performance afresh on each occasion, even though an understanding of the movement quality or intention has been previously decided upon.

Improvisation has been central to both the choreographic and theoretical aspects of the work and the ways these two aspects co-exist and inform each other. As a method, improvisation offers the possibility of an on-going dialogue between the phenomenal and objective dimensions, a dialogue in some ways observable and sometimes reportable.

> *A phenomenology of bodies looks to the ways bodies feel in movement. Not only what muscles and bones are being utilised to move or to dance, but what that feels like. It represents a kind of kinaesthetic sensitivity.* [Rothfield, 1994/5: 80]

A phenomenal orientation to dancing implies that each dancer's experience is different, that their internal understanding will manifest in a unique way. With such an orientation, improvisation has the potential to tap into these experiences and how each dancer embodies his sense of identity. As this work is directed toward the specificities of masculine subjectivity, what Rothfield calls 'kinaesthetic sensitivity', was crucial to realizing the goal in an embodied form. Improvisational dancing, then, provides a methodology for sifting through phenomenal perspectives on dancing and a way of moulding multiple contributions into an objectively constituted performance.

As a choreographer, improvisation is a powerful creative tool. My work, in its initial stages, was forged from repeated improvisational sessions with the dancers. From these sessions emerged themes, ideas, images, relationships and spatial considerations. It is from this rich resource that the content, the structure and, to a certain degree, the intention of the choreography was drawn. The movement parameters (defining the type or quality of movement, how long it lasted, who was involved, and so on) were usually made as a result of testing ideas through improvisation rather than applying a predetermined movement or movement qualities onto the dancers. I would then attempt to clarify or objectify what the dancers would show in a performance. In this sense, there was a link between the subjective origins of improvisation, and the objective imperatives of producing a piece of choreography for public viewing.

These rehearsals became a means of testing ideas gleaned from my own theoretical research. It became a form of physicalized debate and self-reflection, for the dancers and myself, as we engaged with issues pertaining to masculine embodiment and subjectivity. By using discussion and improvisation as the starting points I aimed to create an open and fluid working-environment in which I could experiment, surprises could occur, and to which the dancers could contribute. This creative structure enabled me to operate intuitively throughout, to be open to the unexpected outcomes of improvisation, and to defer any final decisions about the appropriateness and structure of material until close to the performance time. By working intuitively rather than with predetermined directives and ideas, by focusing on the embodied experiences of the men involved and by using the indeterminate quality of improvisation, I aimed to make a dance work that avoided yet commented upon the universalising and domineering capacities of hegemonic masculinity.

The outcome of this process was something of a marriage between the performance, *Chamber*, and a study that charts the interrelated philosophical and artistic processes through which the performance was produced. The result is a dual record – danced and written – of an investigation into how dance might express and reveal masculine subjectivity.

CHAPTER ONE
EMBODYING THEORY

Introduction

This study is aimed at illuminating some of the issues addressed in the making of *Chamber*. The defining themes are parallel concerns that sometimes connect to reveal their common origins and causes. Firstly, there is a dance agenda at play. From the time I started dancing at university I have encountered a mindset that promotes the notion that dancers are generally dumb. The assumption has often been that because dancers spend their time articulating with their bodies rather than with language, they are not intellectually engaged. Consequently, the pursuit of dance has been interpreted as less intellectually demanding than any number of other disciplines, both within different forms of discourse and the arts themselves [Foster, 1996: 7]. This attitude, of course, shows a profound lack of understanding about the processes involved in dancing. But, secondly, it is also representative of attitudes towards bodily culture and embodied practices in general. In other words, the body, and its cultural practices, have been denigrated in Western discourse since the occasion Plato aligned matter with a "...denigrated and imperfect version of the Idea" [Grosz, 1994: 5, see also Bordo, 1998a: 88]. If dance is to be fully valued and understood, this attitude needs to be challenged within the field that originally framed the split between mind and body, namely philosophy. It is in the spirit of this challenge that this work has been articulated.

I have used as the main point of reference and enquiry the work of feminist philosopher and theorist Elizabeth Grosz. Grosz's project, particularly as it is expounded in *Volatile Bodies*, has been to investigate through intensive analysis of major theorists of the body, whether:

> *...subjectivity can be thought...in terms quite other than those implied by various dualisms. Dualism is the belief that there are two mutually exclusive types of "thing", physical and mental, body and mind, that underlies the current preoccupations not only of many philosophers but also of feminist theorists. Feminists, like philosophers, have tended to ignore the body or to place it in the position of being somehow subordinate to and dependent for all that is interesting about it on animating intentions, some sort of physical or social significance. Feminist theory...has tended, with some notable exceptions, to remain uninterested in or unconvinced about the relevance of refocusing on bodies in accounts of subjectivity.* [Grosz, 1994: vii]

Within Grosz's extensive readings of the major theorists of the body, I have used for this project her critique and engagement with the work of French philosopher Maurice Merleau-Ponty. Merleau-Ponty, particularly in his classic *Phenomenology of Perception*, is widely regarded as one of the most sophisticated apologists of embodied subjectivity. His defining theme, put simply, is that subjectivity is always inherently embodied; that the corporeal dimension of perception – perception being the way we as subjects engage with the world – is lived and experienced by us through our bodies. Put another way, his claim is that 'I am my body' [Priest, 1998: 56].

Grosz's reading of Merleau-Ponty is from a feminist perspective and she is critical of aspects of his work. So why chose a feminist theorist's work to locate this performance? It is because, beyond any feminist framing of the body, that the issues she deals with remain inextricably tied to my experiences as a dancer and crucially as a *male* dancer.

The body in philosophy

Before explicating this stance fully, and before I turn to Merleau-Ponty's work in more detail, it would seem appropriate to briefly outline the way in which the human body has been subjugated to the supremacy of mind within the tradition of Western philosophy. Since its origins in ancient Greece, philosophy has been wary of the body and this condition intensified as philosophical thought became unyieldingly wedded to the 'purely conceptual' [Bordo, 1998a: 88]. Early Christianity defined a distinction between man's soul as an immortal God-given entity, and the sinful carnality of the mortal human body. Sin was seen as being corporeally signified and experienced; therefore the body was harshly punished for what were seen as moral inadequacies. Leprosy in the Middle Ages, for example, was seen as the diseased outcome of lechery and covetousness [Grosz, 1994: 5-6].

Susan Hekman, in paraphrasing Susan Bordo, states that "… although Western thought had, since Plato, associated the body with the female and nature, a realm inferior to culture and the male, it was only in the work of Descartes that knowledge itself became masculinized" [Hekman, 1998: 62]. Grosz also credits Descartes with extracting the soul from nature [Grosz, 1994: 6]. Descartes' classification of two substances, a thinking substance (mind) and an extended substance (body) meant only the latter could be attributed a mortal, concrete existence as part of nature and governed by its laws. The mind, or its correlatives soul and consciousness, had no place in nature and existed as a timeless, unchanging truth bearing no similarities to the passionate and misguided whims of the body. It is within this set of principles that Science as a guiding vision was formed; a vision which was Universal, timeless, founded on reason; a vision in which the individual living breathing subject had little importance. The body-subject was defined as historically fixed, natural, passive, mechanistic, needing guidance and ultimately an interference with the more noble workings of the mind.

This split is described as a dualism, but Cartesian dualism is not a neutral or equal designation. An antagonistic relationship exists between the opposing terms and results in a hierarchy of dominance and subordination. The dominant category expels or excludes the coupled term thereby defining itself. The dominant association of 'man' with mind in a patriarchal system, for example, is always accompanied by a suppressed and denigrated 'woman' whose association is with body and nature. By extension, a range of dualistic pairs becomes caught up in this tension where to some extent and in certain contexts, the terms become interchangeable. Terms such as reason and passion, inside and outside, self and other, depth and surface, transcendence and immanence, psychology and physiology, and so on, become implicated in this process. This relationship is the basis for traditional philosophy, indeed most western epistemology, and knowledge within this system are seen as purely conceptual. "As soon as knowledge is seen as purely conceptual, its relations to bodies, the corporeality of both knowers and texts, and the ways these materialities interact must become obscure." [Grosz, 1994: 4]

Many feminists have seen the privileging of mind over body and the consequent expulsion of the latter as one of the defining elements of patriarchal control. To radically summarize this position, women are assigned to the world of the body and nature in a timeless continuum, while men occupy the valued high ground of mind, ideals, or consciousness. The masculine position 'frees' men from the polluting concerns of the body and distances them from the implications of embodiment, thus enabling them to operate as 'pure' entities in the world of ideas and abstract concepts. Elizabeth Grosz sees the body, in this context, "…implicitly defined as unruly, disruptive, in need of direction and judgement, merely incidental to the defining characteristics of mind, reason, or personal identity through its opposition to consciousness, to the psyche and other privileged terms within philosophical thought" [Grosz, 1994: 3].

Certain branches of feminist thought have sought to undermine the essentialist stance which claims the female body to be an inferior, 'natural' phenomenon and therefore historically stable and unchanging. Judith Butler has developed the radical position which altogether denies the existence of any pre-existing agency or capacity for the body beyond what cultural factors ascribe to it [Butler, 1998].

> ...Butler wants to argue for a conception of the body not as the ground of desire, but its occasion and object. "Always already a cultural sign, the body sets limits to the imaginary meanings that it occasions, but it is never free of imaginary construction". Thus the fantasized body cannot be contrasted to the "real" body, or, as in Foucault, pre-discursive sex. It can only be contrasted to another cultural fantasy. [Hekman, 1998: 66-67]

Other feminist theorists such as Susan Bordo have tried to balance Butler's stance by attempting definitions which are inclusive of the body's agency, but as a conditional, culturally coded, historically defined entity [Bordo, 1998a]. Bodies must, according to Bordo, retain some relationship to a 'reality' (materiality); if the body exists only as 'fantasy' then the day-to-day material inequities that female bodies endure as a consequence of the gender imbalance cannot be politically addressed or re-figured [Hekman, 1998: 69, Bordo, 1998a].

Feminism has been particularly successful at including women's experiences (experience being the manner in which the subject, through her body, engages with the world) as a guiding indicator as to the usefulness or appropriateness of theoretical discourse[1]. While the materiality of 'experience' remains a contentious issue, in that it potentially tethers women to the 'fixed' world of bodies, it has remained an important consideration and one that has been carefully and often surprisingly brought to light. For instance, Iris Young's famous article *Throwing like a Girl* brought a phenomenological perspective to an often derided aspect of feminine embodiment with clear political implications; to throw like a girl is substandard compared to the 'power' of men's throwing action [Young, 1998].

Defining Masculinity

A problem emerges in this discussion when trying to shift these understandings to a male context. Attempts to define the term masculinity succinctly encounter a range of difficulties; masculinity as a fixed and unproblematic term of reference cannot be sustained under the intense scrutiny applied to it in relatively recent scholarship. Indeed, as Robert Connell indicates, a key finding of recent sociological research of masculinity is that there is no globally imprinted pattern or globally understood definition [Connell, 2000: 10]. [2] Rather Connell cites various 'masculinities', conditional on factors such as culture, history, nationality, race, class and traditions of gender construction. For example, different cultures have at different historical moments allowed for very different levels of acceptability and participation in homosexual behaviour [Connell, 2000: 10].

In other words, and as feminists such as Elizabeth Grosz have been arguing, gender organization is not a fixed entity. It is mutable and dynamic, not essentially dominated by

---

[1] For an example of writings about representations of the female body, see Suleiman, 1985.
[2] For a more detailed account of new directions in research regarding masculinity and attempts to define the term, see Connell, 2000, Chapters 1 and 2.

human biology. A man does not *need* to behave violently simply because he has the power to do so. For certain men to be encouraged to behave aggressively, as they often are in many activities and social interactions such as sport, they need the support not simply of a biological response but of an entire cultural system which bolsters such behaviour. Men are not born as aggressive entities, but some learn how to behave in this way by engaging in an extremely complex interaction with social forces, institutions, peer groups and so on. Consequently masculinities are primarily defined in cultural arenas, not biological ones [Connell, 2000: 10-13].

However, in most cultures a dominant form of masculinity holds pre-eminence over others. The cultural authority invested in this form creates a situation of dominance and subordination within the masculine gender order.

> *"In most of the situations that have been closely studied there is some hegemonic form of masculinity – the most honoured or desired...The hegemonic form need not be the most common form of masculinity, let alone the most comfortable. Indeed, many men live in a state of some tension with, or distance from, the hegemonic masculinity of their culture or community."* [Connell, 2000: 10-11]

In a patriarchal system gender is presented as dichotomous with masculinity, defined not so much by what it is, but by what it rejects or expels. Practices excluded from hegemonic masculinity, that is all other manifestations of masculinity, are consequently tainted by a symbolic association with femininity [Connell, 2000: 31, Seidler, 1989: 47]. In Western culture, hegemonic masculinity is relentlessly represented by the media image of men as the muscular hero; heterosexual, all-powerful, controlling, driven, and lacking any hint of self-doubt. But men do not live in a world free of contradictions and self-doubt. The marginalisation of all other forms of masculinity by the hegemonic form creates a continuing point of challenge for many men as they attempt to 'live up to' or alternatively avoid the cultural impact of the dominant form. Connell cites the example of a study on male body-builders who would often, in the pursuit of a (heterosexually defined) muscular body and hyper-masculine identification, finance their physical regime by eliciting payment for sex from homosexual men [Connell, 2000: 13]. This tension confirms the inherent contradictions, and problematic qualities surrounding the notion of a fixed and comfortable, all-encompassing masculinity and sexuality [Rutherford, 1988: 22].

However, in situating masculinity as a culturally constructed order, Connell also makes explicit the necessity to acknowledge the materiality of the body. The masculine body cannot be defined as a passive object all men receive or experience in the same way. Bodies are as diverse as the ways in which men are able to use them and these factors must have bearing on how men define their cultural practices. But it is the emphasis on 'practices' which seems crucial here rather than on any presupposed 'natural order' for what men's bodies can or can't do. All practices, which are used to define gender constructions, *refer* to the body and its workings rather than being *determined* by it. Thus, the "...materiality of male bodies matters, not as a template for social masculinities, but as a referent for the configuration of social practices defined as masculinity. Male bodies are what these practices refer to, imply or address" [Connell, 2000: 59].

Masculinity and the experiences of the body

I would emphasize that, given the importance of body-reflexive practice in the construction of gender, remaking of masculinities is necessarily a re-embodiment.
[Connell, 2000: 66]

Bodies have agency and that agency is implicit in the ways men configure and re-configure masculinity. But the patriarchal denial of the body in western societies has meant men have generally distanced themselves from ontological considerations of body but also from bodily practices and expressions, except in a strictly defined and controlled way [Rutherford, 1988: 26]. As such it is acceptable for men to play sport (as long as they don't throw like girls) but it remains problematic for men to dance, this being a 'feminised' and therefore less worthy pursuit. Within hegemonic masculinity, acceptable uses and understandings of men's bodies remains mechanistic; that is to say the body is used as an instrument of extension, valued for what it can do or achieve and how it can be 'trained' to maximize its capabilities. The body is rarely felt or enjoyed and its sensations rarely attended to except in situations of extreme need. It is not seen as having a responsive or distinctive aspect. Emotion, residing as it does in the body, is also suppressed. The object-body is in need of subjugation and this subjugation is accompanied by a "...refusal to acknowledge the distinctive complexities of organic bodies, the fact that bodies construct and in turn are constructed by an interior, a psychical and a signifying view-point, a consciousness or perspective" [Grosz, 1994: 8].

Embedded in *Chamber* is a very personal response to 'masculinity' and my experiences as a male dancer. To be a male dancer in the world in which I grew up and trained as dancer was tantamount to 'coming out', to admitting homosexuality. The revelation of my desire to become a dancer was met by many men and boys with either disgust or admiration – that I could be bold enough to ignore the prevailing ethos of hegemonic acceptability. It is here that the issues of dance as a denigrated feminine practice and the experiences of the male dancer confronting normative masculinity intertwine. To be a male dancer is – in a relatively small way – to confront the kind of prejudice and sexism that feminism has described and detailed for over 30 years. It would be ridiculous and demeaning to the urgencies of feminism to claim I have in any significant way been a victim of sexism. But I have had cause to reflect upon 'what it means to be man', upon my masculinity, and in the face of stiff resistance to the bodily practices that I enjoy and which nourished me. My sympathies for the goals of feminism notwithstanding, it is strategically and politically important for me as a man who enjoys dancing to question a system which demeans this pursuit, and others like it. In this context I have aligned myself in this project with the objectives and theoretical standpoints found within feminism.

The patriarchal construction of hegemonic masculinity remains too tightly bound to easily allow within it dance practices which reflect upon and utilize the experiences of the body. Indeed, masculine experience itself – the very idea of a distinctive realm of experience for men – remains an area only vaguely defined, hidden behind a homogenizing acceptance of 'masculinity' – a kind of unapprised code of silence regarding the differences in the ways men live their lives. This notion states that all masculine experience is equivalent or uniform, and that *experience itself*, with the notable exception of sexual experience, is masculine experience. The term masculine becomes interchangeable with the term universal [Seidler, 1989: 47]. Male subjectivity and the multiplicity of masculine experiences have consequently been rendered invisible by their subsumption under the comforting stasis of an ideal masculinity [Goldstein, 1994: vii, Middleton, 1992: 116-118].

As a consequence of this totalising practice men have never adequately attempted to detail the differences and intricacies of their experiences: experiences which might indicate areas of difference, plurality, divergence and surprise. Masculine experience has been regarded as a given or not regarded at all, but it is only recently that it has been regarded as problematic. [3]

> *Men have functioned as if they represented masculinity only incidentally or only in moments of passion and sexual encounter, while the rest of the time they are representatives of the human, the generic "person". Thus what remains unanalysed, what men can have no distance on, is the mystery, the enigma, the unspoken male body.* [Grosz, 1994: 198]

Clearly if men are to be free to pursue embodied practices outside the realm of the acceptable then they must also attempt to free the body from its negative associations. Part of this task entails detailing what individual experiences men have of their bodies, how they "live" their bodies. Phenomenological reflections on masculine embodiment are required which find the nuances and subtleties beyond the usual iconic or heroic representations of men's bodies. In order for men to discover their bodies within an atmosphere of positive acceptance, men need to relate to their bodies and identify its practices and its becomings as well as the sexual specificities these entail. If, as Grosz states "... the mind is necessarily linked to, perhaps even a part of the body and if bodies themselves are always sexually (and racially) distinct, incapable of being incorporated into a singular universal model, then the very forms that subjectivity takes are not generalizable" [Grosz, 1994: 19]. Men need to extract specific experience from the haze of the universal by particularizing the forms of their subjectivity, and even more of a challenge, by manifesting this in an embodied fashion. One embodied particularity of this project is dancing.

Chamber
Chamber articulates, performs, presents and engages with masculine experience as problematic. In particular it gives body to the experiences of men, aligns men with the body, and identifies their bodily practices and artefacts. The work endeavours to acknowledge that:

> *...a different type of body is produced in and through the different sexual and cultural practices that men undertake. Part of the process of phallicizing the male body, of subordinating the rest of the body to the valorizing functioning of the penis...involves the constitution of the sealed-up, impermeable body... A body that is permeable, that transmits in a circuit, that opens itself up rather than seals itself off, that is prepared to respond as well as initiate, that does not revile its masculinity...or virilize it...would involve a quite radical rethinking of male sexual morphology.* [Grosz, 1994: 200-201]

Dance practices that centre on the experience of the body are explicitly aimed at 'opening up the body', to making it responsive. As a gesture towards rethinking or reformulating the male body, *Chamber* is therefore a questioning of the masculine status quo and the phallocentric systems that govern and control the way men express their physicality and subjectivity. It is not an attempt to illustrate a theory applicable to all men, or to speak for all men. *Chamber* comes with a phenomenological slant driven by the subjective particularities of the men dancing in it, and by myself as maker of it.

---

[3] For a diverse account of how theorists and writers have focused on problems associated with masculine experience, see Goldstein, 1994.

The other assumption pursued in *Chamber* is that subjectivity can be – and for men needs to be – embodied. The phenomenological focus within the making of *Chamber* was on ways in which subjectivity could be constituted corporeally – in dance and movement. Credence has to be given to the life of the body, to functioning within subjectivity and to the interaction between consciousness and physicality.

Merleau-Ponty and the embodied subject

Truth does not 'inhabit' only 'the inner man', or more accurately, there is no inner man, man is in the world, and only in the world does he know himself.
[Merleau-Ponty, 1962: xi]

Maurice Merleau-Ponty's intention in writing *Phenomenology of Perception* was to understand the interconnectedness of interior and exterior, of the world to consciousness. He criticized the necessity within both Idealism and Materialism to posit the subject-object relationship as dichotomous or dualistic.[4] Indeed, as Grosz points out, Merleau-Ponty believed any ontological perspectives that are organized around a binary opposition to be fundamentally incorrect, refusing the "...very terrain and founding pre-suppositions..." [Grosz, 1999: 146] they are built on. For Merleau-Ponty, Grosz writes, the body is never simply an object, indeed to the subject it is never an object at all, but rather it is "...the condition and context through which I am able to have a relation to objects" [Grosz, 1994: 86]. The body is the site from which and through which the subject operates in the world, and as such is not experienced as an object amongst others. My body does not 'stand in front of me' – rather my body "...is always presented to me from the same angle" [Merleau-Ponty, 1962: 90]. In other words, the body provides the subject with the horizon and perspectival point of origin in relation to the world that makes interaction with other objects and subjects possible [Priest, 1998].

As such we experience the world through our bodies, through the receptive and perceptive capabilities they possess. We 'live' our bodies unable to detach ourselves from the experiential immersion this presupposes. Our bodies are embedded in the world and our relationship with other objects is mediated through our bodies. Detached reflection, as a way of understanding the information received by the body, is impossible. Knowledge of the body, and conversely of the world, is only attainable and therefore made cognizant and meaningful, by the subject engaging with the world as a physical entity. Within this operation consciousness cannot act as a pure entity, distinct from, yet directing and interpreting, the necessities of an inert body. This would entail an existential impossibility.

The perceiving mind is an incarnated body. I have tried... to re-establish the roots of mind in its body and in its world, going against the doctrines which treat perception as a simple result of the action of external things on our body as well as against those which insist on the autonomy of consciousness. These philosophies commonly forget – in favour of a pure interiority – the insertion of the mind in corporeality, the ambiguous relation with our body, and correlatively, with perceived things... And it is equally clear that one does not account for the facts by superimposing a pure, contemplative consciousness on a thing-like body... perceptual behaviour emerges... from relations to a situation and to an environment which are not merely the workings of a pure, knowing subject
[Merleau-Ponty, 1964: 3-4]

---

[4] Idealism is the doctrine that sees the subject as constituted exclusively as mind or consciousness with the physical facts as essentially irrelevant. Materialism sees the person as a complex object with the contents of consciousness dependent on its physical facts. (See Priest, 1998: 57)

All meaning or understanding about the world and all intellectual activity is given form by the active differentiation and perceptual organization the body undertakes as it interacts with other objects.

Merleau-Ponty tried to exemplify the interconnectedness of the psychical and the physical by referring to case studies of neurological disturbance in brain damaged patients. His thesis was that certain disorders, such as agnosia and phantom limb syndrome, are neither exclusively physiological nor exclusively psychological but stem from the disintegration of interaction between the two.[5] Merleau-Ponty used in detail the famous case study of the brain damaged aphasic patient Schneider, drawn from the work of Goldstein and Gelb.[6] Schneider lacked the ability to operate in the abstract, despite having lost no motor, sensory or requisite intellectual abilities (although impairment was certainly present). Only concrete, goal-oriented tasks were possible for him as he lacked any ability to project his thoughts or wishes into a future context. Only the present is accessible to him:

> *For example he is able to take out his handkerchief from his pocket and blow his nose but is unable to perform these same actions with his eyes shut. He is unable to perform any action or respond to any situation which is not currently present. He can only perform actions by watching his limbs in movement. He is incapable of imitating any action unless he is called to do so by something external.* [Grosz, 1994: 89]

Grosz asserts that by his examination of these cases of neurological disorder, Merleau-Ponty showed that while traditional psychology and physiology presumed a fundamentally passive body, the two dimensions of body and mind are in fact irreducible. Neither motor skills nor the requisite mental capacity to achieve abstract tasks were absent in Schneider. Instead he lacked the capacity to communicate across these two areas and a system which organized his mental and physical capacities into a functioning whole. Merleau-Ponty's appraisal indicated that the body's way of organizing itself as it moves through the world is constructed outside of exclusively neurological considerations. Rather, experiences are negotiated not merely by raw physical necessity, but also by our expectations of the situation and the different meaning objects have for the body's movements and capabilities.

This idea is encapsulated in the concept of body image or body schema Merleau-Ponty borrowed from psychoanalysts and neurologists (Schilder, Lacan) and developed to his own ends [Grosz, 1994: 91-92].[7]

> *The body is able to move, to initiate and undertake actions, because the body schema is a series, or rather a field, of possible actions, plans for action, maps of possible movements the body "knows" how to perform. The body schema is also a field in which the subject's cohesion and identity as a subject and its intimate incarnation in and as a particular body take place.* [Grosz, 1994: 95]

---

[5] Grosz has described the conditions of agnosia and phantom limb syndrome as follows: "In the phantom limb... the patient still suffers a pain in a location where the limb used to be, before its amputation; agnosia... is the nonrecognition of a part of the body as one's own. The phantom limb illustrates an organ or bodily part within a total body image that is no longer there; agnosia by contrast is the nonrecognition of a body part that should occupy a position within the body image." [Grosz, 1994: 89]

[6] Grosz outlines a detailed discussion of the work of brain researchers such as Goldstein and Gelb and their input to ideas about body image (Grosz, 1994: 62-85).

[7] For a summary of Schilder's formulation of the concept of body image, see Grosz (1994: 83).

An individual's understanding of their body image is the precondition for their being able to negotiate or understand space and the objects within that space. We do not understand spatiality directly through our senses but through our bodily situation. We perceive space as a relationship between an internal, yet perpetually central, organizing perspective (consciousness) and the series of objectively located points in space (objects), thus putting these two into the same perceptual field and allowing us to interrelate with other objects. The body is the unchanging location for this perspective, the point of origin for all experience we have of the world. For a subject to exist in the world, to have knowledge of the world, to have knowledge of the self in relation to the world and interrelate with other subjects and objects, he/she must do so as an *embodied* subject.

The body also moves in and through space mediated by the 'body image'. Body image is complicated, dynamic, changeable and fundamental to any understanding of lived space and lived time. Yet our bodies do not do so consciously. We function on a physiological level independent of any 'knowledge' of this physiology. We 'do' physical tasks: we move or we 'feel' movement for the most part completely separated from the specific knowledge of the mechanics of such movement. And because we act or move in accordance with the unique manifestations of our own body image, how we move will ultimately be subjectively articulated and realized.

> Our body is not in space like things; it inhabits or haunts space. It applies itself to space like a hand to an instrument, and when we wish to move about we do not move the body as we move an object. We transport it without instruments...since it is ours and because, through it, we have access to space. [Merleau-Ponty, 1964: 5]

The Dancing Subject

Merleau-Ponty is potentially important to dance because he extinguishes the dichotomous privileging of the manifestations of the mind over those of the body. Body becomes central to all existence and interaction with the world and consequently practices which are experiential or give expression to the body can be viewed in a more positive light. Dance in this equation becomes important and worthy of attention; not secondary or even irrelevant to the explorations of the mind. As a result, knowledge does not remain exclusive, unassailable nor removed from the experiences of dancing. Dancing *is* a way of knowing and as such gives experiential dimension to the self. This 'knowing' is no less configured and shaped by the cultural dimension because of its physical dimension. Dance is not an essentialist statement – the body is as culturally defined as anything else – rather, dancing requires that the agency of the body be given credit also. This is the domain of what Mabel Todd called 'the thinking body' [Todd: 1937]. It is an interaction between mind and body, an entwining of the two, both with degrees of agency but, importantly, with aspects of bodily experience unfathomable by the operations of the mind. Further, it is argued in this understanding that "... Merleau-Ponty establishes the possibility for the body as an opponent to the dominance of the sign. The body, as the container of an experience not directly apprehensible by mind, carves an arena of autonomy from what has otherwise been considered a ubiquitous force" [Martin, 1990: 34].

> The self known in dance moves beyond the limits of our mental cognito. We dance to become acquainted with that which cannot be known by any other means – to find out what can be known through the body as a mental, physical, spiritual whole. Thus we acquire a kind of knowledge we might designate as experiential. Indeed, we commonly speak of skill in dance as a form of knowledge and also

speak of kinaesthetic intelligence as an aspect of skilful dancing. But dance involves more than just knowing how to do a movement. It also involves knowing how to express the aesthetic intent of a movement and how to create aesthetic movement imagery. All of these forms of knowing how are forms of bodily lived (experiential) knowledge. As such they are avenues for self-knowledge. [Fraleigh, 1987: 26]

Sondra Horton Fraleigh, while claiming the possibility of a "lived wholeness of the self in dance", acknowledges the presence of a dialectical dualism in dance [Fraleigh, 1987: 12]. The mind, she observes, cannot always adequately comprehend the nature of embodiment, while tending towards objectifying or distancing itself from the experience of embodiment. For example, a dancer must objectify the operation of their body in order to meet the choreographic dictates of a choreographer's work. A dancer must 'learn the steps' before being able to develop any personal understanding of how the movement works on their body. Only once the movement has been fully understood, fully embodied, can the psychic distance between the objective and subjective body dissolve.

Indeed, dance has often been a willing participant in the separation of mind and body. The body in dance is often regarded as an 'instrument' which needs to be shaped and trained into the requisite, objectively ordered movement patterning. In this mechanistic approach to dancing the mind is the master, (fiercely) controlling the body, always pushing it to do bigger, more spectacular feats. Clearly, dualism at the site of the body is possible or even necessary. The relationship is domineering with the body regarded as 'merely physical' and of lesser importance than the thoughts, feelings and aspirations it is being driven to represent.

Dancing may use strategies which objectify the body's potential as a means to an end, such as learning a choreographer's work, but this is *intentional* and not based on a belief of any fundamental dualism. Dancing which acknowledges the phenomenal qualities of the body differs from these conventional practices. Fraleigh articulates the belief in the fundamental interaction inherent in such dancing:

Lived-body theory provides a means toward overcoming dualistic concepts of dance, which regard the body as an instrument, movement as the medium, and mind or soul as the mover or motivational source for dance. Lived-body concepts hold that the body is lived as a body-of-action. Human movement is the actualisation, the realization, of embodiment. Movement cannot be considered as medium apart from an understanding that movement is body, not just something that the body accomplishes instrumentally as it is moved by some distinct, inner, and separable agency. Embodiment is not passive; it is articulate. In other words, I live my body as a body-of-motion, just as I also live my self in motion. Body, movement, self and agency...are ultimately not separable entities, which is not to say dualisms (or dialectics) may not appear in consciousness within certain contexts. Thus we might recognize phenomenal (lived) dualisms without accepting metaphysical dualism. [Fraleigh, 1987: 13]

Conclusion

If we accept that men have not adequately articulated the experiences that give shape to the nuances of masculinity, particularly with regard to the male body, then dancing offers just that possibility. If we also accept that masculinity needs to be reformulated and therefore (re)embodied in order for the hegemonic model to be challenged, then the 'feminised' pursuit of dancing offers a powerful opportunity for this to happen. Dancing is necessarily embodied and requires that the dancer 'feel' the movement, not think it. It requires him to experience his body, not as armament, but as intelligent, responsive and dynamic. An instrumental approach to the dancing in a project such as this would be an anathema. All masculine dance can be a challenge to a patriarchal economy but more powerfully so, if it can be done by men who are fully aware of the political implications of what they are doing. Indeed, it calls for a conscious political decision to do so; the political dimension cannot be circumnavigated. If men who dance and choreograph insist on portraying men in dance only as 'strong' and 'muscular', analogous to the macho hero in movie making, then they are failing to acknowledge the issue. If men in dance insist on making male dancing 'acceptable' by continually virilizing their activity, then the act is one of compliance to the patriarchal demands. Men will have failed to create a dynamic, felt, specific, embodied practice to reconfigure masculinity into multitude ways of moving; ones that reflect the multiple differences in men's lives.

CHAPTER TWO
SITUATING PRACTICE

Introduction
In considering how I as a dance artist (and this project) relate to the dance field it seems necessary to attempt to define what constitutes the 'field'. The process of placing ones work or ideas in the context of national or international developments has specific ramifications when considering dance practice. Unlike most academic or literary disciplines, gaining an understanding of dance in its current and past practice is limited, I believe, to that which is seen or experienced in performance or in practice. To *read* about a choreographer's work and ideas is to receive a distorted impression of their work mediated by the subjective and often unsatisfactory description or interpretation by a third party – the critic or observer. Even a choreographer writing about their own work can only ever preface, conceptualise or expand on the choreography itself. The ultimate understanding relies on the reader having experienced the kinaesthetic dimension of dancer's bodies moving through time and space.

By extension, and from a choreographer's point of view, to fully understand another artist's movement style and its relationship to their own work one must have some experience of it. For example, I know from reading about Steve Paxton that he has a certain philosophical outlook on dance and performance that is improvisational, anti-spectacular, non-elitist and aims for complicity with the audience. These are all interesting and valuable philosophical tenets, which could inform my work. However, until I see his work in performance or, even better, do a workshop with him, I will never have anything other than an abstract understanding of his ideas with no real concept of the way he moves. However, if I was to *do* his work I would then understand how his way of moving differs from my own, what aspects of his work I have difficulty with and how my own work might then be extended. In other words placing myself in relation to Steve Paxton would be impossible to do without embodying his work in some way. For a choreographer to place him/herself in the field thus implies an embodied field, a field of their own experience. To do otherwise would be to dilute the original intentions of the choreographer being researched.[8]

Despite these difficulties it remains important that I attempt to locate my practice in an artistic context which might serve to illuminate the aims of this project. Within the field of dance the work of Lloyd Newson and Steve Paxton, two internationally recognized dance makers, has been involved in very different ways to bring attention to issues confronting masculinity. In using Newson and Paxton as points of reference I have been particularly interested in their philosophical intentions of their work. The aesthetic comparison, a comparison of dance styles, has seemed less integral to this process than in attempting to understand why they do what they do. While this may seem like a contradiction (thought privileged over the movement itself) this is because of two factors. Firstly, I have not been able to adequately understand the aesthetic fabric of their respective bodies of work because I have not had sufficient embodied or participatory experience of it. This is particularly true of Paxton, which I have not seen (although I have danced with, studied with or seen artists who have worked with Paxton – the embodied lineage of dance). In conjunction with this is the fact that *Chamber* is, for the most part, improvised by other dancers whose connection to these two choreographers varies

---

[8] Even watching dance on video or film is far from an accurate representation of the 'live' event. While the shapes the dancers make in space and the style of movement are clear, much of the original intention is lost in the filming of a live performance. The camera (or cameraperson) decides how the work will be viewed. If the entire space and all the dancers are in picture then intimate moments become difficult to discern. If a close up is used on, say, a duet the viewer has no sense of how this is placed within the whole. The energetic qualities, facial expressions, dancers' breathing and most importantly, kinaesthetic stimulus, are lost in this flat, two-dimensional representation. It is impossible to fully 'know' what the work is like. You are required to trust the judgement of a camera to provide a full and adequate understanding of the event.

significantly. Consequently my examination of the two choreographers lies with what they say about their work and how they perceive their intentions.

Lloyd Newson and Steve Paxton come from very different dance traditions and aesthetics but have both been fundamental in initiating debate and responding to social concerns about the constructions of what it means to be a man. I have been interested in the ways in which they negotiate such concerns in dance and how they confront traditional dualities of masculine/feminine and body/mind. Yet their work could be viewed as antithetical to one another; Newson's emphasizes representational forms of performance, while Paxton has been committed to the notion that dancing needs no other referent than itself. It is certainly too simplistic to define them in this way alone, as both artists have been actively seeking ways of diminishing the divide between traditional dualities of man/woman, mind/body and nature/culture. But I shall attempt to use this potential for antithesis between Newson and Paxton to frame this project and the dualities it both contains and comments on.

One of the underlying premises for *Chamber* has been that alternative expressions or constructions of masculinity need to be acknowledged, embodied and presented. However, this ideal exists within a choreographic framework of often restrictive representations of hegemonic masculinity. It is because of these two conflicting directions within *Chamber* that the work of Newson and Paxton provides useful points of reference within the spectrum I have outlined.

Lloyd Newson
Lloyd Newson's considerable reputation (and that of his London-based Company DV8 Physical Theatre) rests with his uncompromising 'issue-based' performance pieces that centre on the behavioural motivations of the protagonists. His work has often dealt directly with issues pertaining to masculinity, particularly homosexuality and homophobia, and masculine aggression and violence. Works such as *My Sex, Our Dance* (1986), *Dead Dreams of Monochrome Men* (1988), and *Enter Achilles* (1995) have all dealt specifically with various manifestations of masculine identity, particularly homosexual identity. The three works involved all-male casts and arose out of the politically motivated drive to bring gay rights and homophobia into full public view. Underlying Newson's intentions in spotlighting often-taboo subject matter has been his political commitment to undermining 'fortress masculinity'. In order to give expression to the alternative masculine identities that are part of the gay community (of which Newson is a part) he has sought to present normative masculinity as problematic and psychologically complex, even contradictory. Homosexuality has also been presented in DV8's work as a product of this defensive and repressive patriarchal domination. His attack on the acceptable and accepted has consequently been an attempt to create permission for alternative expressions of masculinity to exist [Burt, 1995].

Newson's first work to come to major attention was *My Sex, Our Dance*, which was a response to the increasing threat for gay men posed by the spread of HIV/Aids. As well as this it was a bold depiction of homosexual sexuality and the restrictions gay men were forced to operate within in an increasingly homophobic environment. The work, a duet for Nigel Charnock and Newson himself, combined a frenetic and acrobatic physicality with moments of seemingly dysfunctional intimacy. In choreographic terms it uses "…an analogy of physical risk-taking to explore how far two men can trust each other. How far can a body, somebody, the 'body', be pushed before it becomes dangerous [Luckhurst, 1997]?

Developed by examining situations in which they became violent in their own lives, the two performers repeatedly fling themselves at one another seemingly trapped in a cycle of violence, yet craving intimacy. When the work was first performed in 1986 it succeeded in raising powerful questions about homosexual identity and sexuality, and gave dance in England a potent political voice [Luckhurst, 1997]?

Dead Dreams of Monochrome Men (1988) is perhaps DV8's most forceful work. The work was made and first performed when the media's attack on homosexuality (as the 'cause' of the Aids epidemic) was at its zenith in Britain. The British government had introduced the infamous Clause 28 (1988 Local Government Bill) making it illegal for local government authorities to knowingly promote homosexuality. The political stance taken by Newson in Our Sex, My Dance was continued with *Dead Dreams of Monochrome Men*. This was a chilling response to the book Killing for Company, by Brian Masters, based on the life of homosexual mass murderer Dennis Nilsen. *Dead Dreams of Monochrome Men* was not directly about the book but was based on improvisations conducted by the four male dancers in response to the book. The work is full of bleak, angry and aggressive imagery. It reflected the *"...loneliness and hollowness that results when gay or straight men are unable to form meaningful relationships, and uses the presentation of sado-masochist situations as a way in which to explore this"* [Burt, 1995: 188].

Newson contends that it is the subject matter that determines the qualities of the movement and has been highly critical of the self-referential and abstract tendencies of formalist contemporary dance. Newson states:

> *One of the things which distinguishes DV8's work for me is that it's dance about something. One of my concerns in forming DV8 was to broaden the perspective of dance and try to make it more relevant to people's lives. I prefer the term 'movement' to 'dance' because I feel that dance is only one type of movement. That's another reason we call ourselves Physical Theatre, not a dance company: because I think the word dance has many limiting associations.*

> *Too often I see dance companies who are more interested in the aesthetic and the visual than they are in content. Ironically enough, I think any aesthetic is political, but unfortunately a lot of people don't take that on board. People refer to DV8 dealing with sexual politics: the Royal Ballet deals with sexual politics, it's just conservative rather than radical or questioning.* [Tushingham, 1995]

The kind of movement DV8 employs is certainly different from many formalist choreographers and has been influential in making contemporary dance more theatrically driven. It is movement that seeks direct relationships to narratives and to social and cultural contexts (men dancing boisterously in a pub in *Enter Achilles*). Newson has also attempted to open the tightly delineated range of acceptability for body-shape and age in dance. He argues:

> *Why do older performers decide not to stay in dance? It's not only about the deterioration of the body. Too many of those working in dance are concerned with youth and beauty, with making pretty pictures and shapes. Rarely does dance address the complexities of the real world. At times dance feels very juvenile to me: until we re-define our notions of what dance is, what a dancer looks like and how a dancer moves; until older, fat and disabled dancers can be encouraged to keep performing and to talk about their lives, the form will remain young and*

immature. We must encourage dancers to use more than just their bodies.
[Luckhurst, 1997]

Yet each of these works dissecting masculinity have been marked, even defined at some point, by an extreme, 'high-risk' physicality. The metaphor seems consistently to be that male-to-male relationships are fraught and dangerous. Consequently the aesthetic, emotional tenor and movement qualities are defined in aggressive, athletic, strength-orientated ways. This has the potential to offer the male dancers (and in works which focus on masculinity) only the kind of dancing which fits the traditional expectations of what is appropriate physical expression for a man. Dance has traditionally held that men should look active and powerful to avoid any association with the 'softness' of the feminine aspect with which dance is usually associated.[9]

The exception to this in *Enter Achilles* is the dance by the (gay) stranger ('other') upon entering the pub (male domain). His dance is soft, fluid, self-absorbed and beautiful. His reward for such an open display, are threats of violence by the other men. Clearly *Enter Achilles* is commenting on this socio-sexual status quo: Gay men are 'in touch with their feminine sides' while straight men repress them. Newson's actual intentions were clearly not so singular, however:

> *...in* Enter Achilles *we did a whole range of improvisations based on what is acceptable male physical contact, about what is considered an acceptable way for a man to walk, to talk. We played with the simple idea of straight and bent movements, how these affected how we felt and how they were perceived externally. We looked at the pressures on men to play particular sports, we'd talk about relationships with our fathers, our mothers, our best male friends, what we expect from them, and how that differs from our relationships with our female friends...and then we would get to specifics, because you generalise and make all these theories but it's the specifics that are interesting. In the end, the interest lies not so much in how we do it, but in how he does it, and how specifics can often contradict theories, and are often very conflicting, and how that becomes human, complex and revealing.* [Butterworth, 1998]

Yet being made aware of this specificity or complexity was not how I responded to *Enter Achilles*. I would argue that in terms of the quality or range of movement it was more forceful in its adherence to the *norms* of masculinity. In my perception of this work no alternatives are presented for the heterosexual men; no space is allowed which a less-fixed definition of masculinity can emerge. The straight men are confined yet again to the conformity of thoughtless brutality and displays of power. The power of Newson's work for me rests with his exposure of the brutality of the stereotype, not in an exploration of alternatives. In *Dead Dreams* the gay image of sado-masochist behaviour has distorted the stereotype beyond the normative into the abject. It seeks to identify and expose the manifestations of the repression that closet gay men. But the work is an angry political scream about what can happen in a repressive society, about the ways things are. Despite the impact and political value of this work, it is reactive rather than visionary and makes no gesture towards alternative ways of being for men.

As image-based, physical theatre DV8's work presents powerful representational perspectives on social and political issues. These are often presented from the point of view of individuals.

---

[9] For a history of this relationship see Chapter One of Burt, 1995.

I really don't see a difference between what is personal and what is political, and therefore I prefer to look at the individual's actions, responsibilities, and how they reflect on the larger political, sociological, psychological arena...[DV8's work] delves into how individuals relate to one another emotionally and intellectually, rather than being about movement patterns, design patterns, like human moving wallpaper. [Butterworth, 1998]

Newson's emphasis on representation is based on the individual's psychological or behavioural responses to the world. In this emphasis though, it is the person's consciousness that seems to be privileged, with his works dissecting the psychological impulses of the protagonists. One gets the impression that their physicality is only important in as much as it is a sign of what is happening to them psychologically, rather than as dance which is understood in its own terms. Newson again:

My background in psychology has provoked me constantly to ask "why?" Why do an arabesque? What does an arabesque mean? ...I left traditional dance because of its lack of specificity, its lack of questioning and its lack of rigour beyond technique. Psychology training has helped me to see patterns of behaviour and language and think of physical ways to interpret these. [Luckhurst, 1997]

By stressing the importance of the body purely as symbolic of the machinations of consciousness have we not returned to the classic mind/body dichotomy, with mind again dominant? In the context of work which examines the operations of masculinity (and by extension its part in maintaining patriarchy) this would seem to be a potentially retrograde strategy.

Again, one could argue that Newson has merely mirrored the world in which we live and re-presents it provocatively. But, if the body is to resonate on its own terms it cannot be denigrated. Dance, particularly, should respect the alternative logic that the body can offer and not dismiss the moving body as devoid of meaning. Its meaning, however, is often not best represented by language.

I would hope that dance is more than acrobatics. Yet to a large extent it ends up being about what you can do with your body alone – that becomes its preoccupation. DV8's preoccupation is: if the leg is thrown up beside the ear, why is it there? There must be a reason for it, not just "Look at what we're able to do: look how high I can kick my leg". [Tushingham, 1995]

When Newson says it must 'mean something' does he mean it must be able to be interpreted from within the logical operations of language, or with reference to the symbolic order? This insistence on logocentricity seems to sideline the indefinable, ephemeral experiences of the moving body.

Steve Paxton

It is this experience of the body with which Steve Paxton has been primarily connected. His approach has centred on subjective, experiential responses to time, gravity and anatomy. Each individual's internal understanding of these elements within a dynamic and shifting physiological field determines how they will dance. It is not how the dancing 'looks' but how it 'feels' that is privileged; not an insistence on 'being like' something, just 'being' that is of primary importance.

As a proponent of the radical social and political milieu of the 1960s, Paxton sought connections between the egalitarian ideals of the time and his artistic practice. Consequently, he and other dancers of this era (such as the Judson Church group with which Paxton was aligned) attempted to undermine traditional dance forms, particularly if these forms were out of step with the social ethos of the day. The elitist stance of the virtuoso dancer was replaced with the pedestrian body performing Merce Cunningham's maxim 'any movement can be dance'. Paxton's 1960s choreography was primarily defined by the act of walking. His *Satisfyin'* *Lover*, first shown in 1967, has been performed at various times by groups of between 30 – 84 people. In it the performers walk in a prearranged sequence, one by one or as groups, from one side of the performance space to the other, and then exit. It is a celebration of the ordinary: ordinary bodies of all shapes and sizes, anti-choreographic, anti-technical, achievable by anyone. Yet it was this attention to the mundane that traditional modern dance found so threatening; the processes of democracy embodied in such simplicity was an affront to the heroic, elitist symbolism of the Graham era [Burt, 1995].

From the early 1970s on, Paxton chose to work exclusively with improvisational dancing. He was a member of the Grand Union collective (1970-1976) whose improvised performances spanned movement, dance and theatre in a free-form spontaneous anarchy. But in 1972 he began working with a group of 11 men (athletes, students) who later performed the seminal *Magnesium* at Oberlin College. Cynthia Novack describes the improvised but 'scored' performance: [10]

> *Performing on several wrestling mats, the men stagger about, crash into each* > *other, fall, roll, and get up only to lurch around again. A lot of hand-clasping and* > *pulling or dragging occurs, so that the dance looks like drunken wrestling at* > *times. The performers have no orientation to the audience toward the audience,* > *pursuing their falling with a task-like attitude.* [Novack, 1990: 61]

What emerged from this period of exploration (and later refined) was the form termed 'contact improvisation'. A great deal of grassroots fervour had been created in the USA by feminist groups and their stance, which in turn prompted many American men to form men's groups and examine 'masculine roles'. These groups tackled issues such as the ways men could interact without being competitive, promote non-sexual intimacy, gender equality and so on. Paxton, caught up in the spirit of the times, worked with a group of men on such issues creating "…dance material, contemporary with this cultural concern, [but] not inextricably bound to it" [Banes, 1980: 64]. Perhaps also in response to the 'anything goes' openness of the Grand Union performances, Paxton's focus for contact improvisation was, initially, tightly defined by the relationship of giving and receiving body weight, and sensitivity to the 'point of contact' between participants. This was to counter what Paxton perceived as a tendency of the Grand Union method to isolate its individual members [Novack, 1990: 60-61].

Paxton has consistently maintained that the complexity of the body has been lost in western culture and that this has been aligned to a disregard for the 'natural' status the body (as he sees it) necessarily holds. For Paxton the "…sedentary insanity of this culture" has resulted in a lack

---

[10] A 'score' in dance terms defines an instruction (or instructions) for the dancers to follow in which they attempt to embody this image or task but without having a predetermined series of movements or steps. It implies a loose structure for the dancers to improvise within.

of responsiveness to both the body and its place in the natural world. As the person principally credited with formulating contact improvisation, Paxton was, in part, driven by this loss:

> *To me what was lost was the chance to be throwing yourself around in an environment and developing other centres in the brain for our survival: we needed sphericity, we needed climbing, we needed swimming...We needed the senses to open to an extraordinary degree in order to be as aware of the surroundings as possible, and to be able to maintain that with a kind of Zen-like attention. [Lori b, 1996: 47]*

This is a plea for balance in a society dominated by systems and institutions that restrain the body and curtail its potential. It is a philosophy which reflects its roots in the activism and the desire for social change of the 1960s. Contact improvisation has developed into a profoundly social form, requiring complex interpersonal communication and interaction to be fluidly and efficiently negotiated. It requires its participants to be responsive not only to their own bodies but also to the point of connection with another's. This exchange is set within the ever-changing physical topography created by the giving and receiving of each other's weight.

This concern for sensory awareness is equally present in Paxton's solo improvisational work. How the body is known in movement, or a physical event measured by a dancer, is subjective. It is our 'feeling' for our body weight that determines how we use it. Equally it is a subjective rather than quantifiable sense of time that determines how long we follow a movement when improvising. In discussing scientific or positivist approaches to sensory analysis Paxton says:

> *"...most of their [sensory analysts] work on the senses relates to those of the surface, disregarding questions about our sense of gravity, our feeling of the muscles of the body when they are quiet, or the sense of 'being', if I may propose such a sense."* [Paxton, 1992: 126]

In readying participants for contact improvisation Paxton developed an exercise he calls 'the small dance' or 'standing'. He invites the dancers to stand, with his eyes closed, and prompts them to follow internal physical sensations and allow the voluntary muscles to relax.

> *Then after I have gone over the whole body and they have been standing for a while, I say, "Feel the small dance". The skeletal muscles are holding you up – right and there is a point where you can balance inside the small dance, where everything equalizes out. It's a place of balance where the skeletal muscles don't seem to know what to do exactly, or don't need to do anything. So the forces of the body are equalized. It's such a delicate moment that if you even think "Ah it's happened" it pushes you out of it. So you have to suspend your thinking, you have to become habituated to it. And then, it's an amazing feeling because one is used to strains and stresses and pulls and movements in the body – it's part of one's habitual awareness – and suddenly there's no discernable muscular activity, in that state of balance. [Paxton, 1977: 3]*

This state casts the participant into movement. What is of primary importance in the 'small dance' and what generates any movement are the unique physical interpretations each dancer makes of these sensations, and how this 'state of balance' is given subjective expression. This microanalysis of the experiential life of the body is an approach shared by other proponents of 'release technique' whose aim is to 'let' the body move, to 'allow' rather than 'make', in a state of heightened internal physical awareness. If movement is initiated from the skeletal muscles the body's range of movement is enhanced and more open, and less reliant on patterns of the habitual. There are no expectations about the articulation of the movement: no templates, no predetermined shapes and nothing to copy. In this indeterminacy each dancer is credited with making choices about how they want to move, transferring authority to each moving body, rather than issuing from a teacher/choreographer.

It is also an approach that denies the prominence of vision. Vision has been strongly associated with the modernist patriarchal agendas of order, unity and aesthetic control (after all, dancers should look a certain way). In Paxton's kind of dance, the dancers cannot look at a model of how the movement should be executed (by following the teacher or choreographer). Such an approach removes the judgmental 'stick' of vision, allowing dancers to feel their own way through a dancing moment. Paxton postulates, "For many people vision is a kind of tool which reaches out and grabs things...It's a probing instrument. For other people, it's a receptive instrument...Peripheral vision training is partly to allow the world to enter, because it is softer, not so much a tool as focus is. Peripheral vision is more apt to allow you to hear and feel" [Paxton in Williams, 1996: 32]. In contact improvisation the shared dancing also hinges on the understanding communicated through the sense of touch. Again vision is de-emphasised in order "...to entertain in coexistence both activity and passivity, mind and body, self and other" [Williams, 1996: 31].

While his work usually does not explicitly address masculinity as subject matter, Paxton's dancing and his approach to dancing have consistently undermined traditional expectations of the male dancer. Ramsay Burt also argues that Paxton's solo work is much more radical in its challenge to traditional masculinity than contact improvisation. Burt contends that contact improvisation, despite its acknowledged value, still offers men the opportunity to be seen as risk-takers in an environment where physical prowess is highly valued. Whereas, "Paxton's own dancing invariably presents unconventional uses of the body which challenge the spectator to reassess aspects of masculine identity and experience that are generally denied or rendered invisible in mainstream cultural forms" [Burt, 1995: 148]. As examples of this Burt cites *Flat* (1964) in which Paxton walked in a rectangular path around the performance space, occasionally stopping or pretending to sit (there was no chair). After doing this he removed one article of clothing at a time and hung them on one of three hooks taped to his chest. He continued to remove each piece of clothing, walking in-between, until he was left in his underwear. The image of a male 'clothes-horse', an effigy relentlessly assigned to women, is cited by Burt as a radical challenge to masculine identity. Paxton refuses to develop the movement beyond the pedestrian with no build to climax. Avoiding the audience's gaze he sidesteps any reference to the heroic or the need to prove himself in masculinist terms.

Paxton's solo improvisations have also played with the range of movement qualities that are acceptable for the male dancer. Since 1973 he has presented solo improvisations under the title *Dancing*, and from 1986 *Goldberg Variations*. These have been rich in movement, always striving for the spontaneous and the unexpected:

> *There is a quiet, surprising pleasure in watching Paxton experiment with relations between body parts, and with images of body states like strength and illness...One sees combinations and body attitudes that are unusual for dancing, sometimes even for any activity in our culture. Yet they look satisfying, organic, not like copied images of unusual postures, but like movements and positions arrived at naturally in the course of an uncensored, intelligent flow of energy and weight*

through the skeletal and muscular systems. One sometimes recognizes the shapes as images from other contexts: sports, medicine, ballet, drunkenness, modern dance, sculpture, painting, nature. But the imagery is fleeting. What remains is a continuing sense of the body's potential to invent and discover, to recover equilibrium after losing control, to regain vigor despite pain and disorder. Paxton's dancing tells us that... the body's grace is rooted in its extraordinary varied repertoire of capabilities. [Banes, 1980: 70]

Paxton's improvisation seems to give dimension to the claim that subjectivity is indeed of the body; that the body is a repository of identity. The lines between what Paxton thinks, feels and does seem less distinct here. "Properties often associated with mind...intelligence, judgement, communication – and with the emotions – tenderness, expression, spontaneity – are attributed to the body, thereby blurring commonly accepted categorizations of aspects of a person." [Novack, 1990: 185] This emphasis aligns masculinity with the body in ways potentially confronting to normative masculine identity.

This work is not easy to categorize, contain or describe. Paxton's improvisations defy adequate description; language does not do them justice. They are fleeting and indeterminate making it difficult to situate them in fixed or absolute terms. The conventions of choreography do not always comfortably apply to improvisation. If structure or form is established, it may be abandoned as the impulse changes tack. This placement, outside of order and fixity, toys with the masculine desire to attribute symbolic significance. Intention and representation do not necessarily become the key determinants in establishing meaning; instead another kind of logic is being asked for. It is logic rooted in the kinaesthetic appreciation of dancing, but is only in tenuous dialogue with the logocentric (the body remains culturally coded). As Steve Paxton himself contends: "Improvisation is a word for something which can't keep a name; if it does stick around long enough to acquire a name, it has begun to move towards fixity. Improvisation tends in that direction. Dance is the art of taking place. Improvisational dance finds the places." [Paxton, 1992: 129]

Conclusion

"I write woman: woman must write woman. And man, man... it's up to him to say where his masculinity and femininity are at: this will concern us when men have opened their eyes and seen themselves clearly." Helene Cixous *The Laugh Of The Medusa*

A key tenet of this project is that the masculine aspect dominates in Western social, cultural and interpersonal relations. It is a domination that has tangible negative implications for women as well as men, and needs to be challenged. Maligned because of its embodied status, dance itself is equally caught up in the mire. Furthermore and by a strange reversal of association, male dancers come to be feminised also, deserving of suspicion because of their collusion with practices of the (feminine) body. However, this assumption is challenged here not as a didactic affront to masculinity but as a series of questions. What is masculine experience? How can this be embodied? These questions seek to catch sight of what has been rendered invisible by force of cultural habit and prejudice, but without the expectation of crystalline clarity. It seems enough that the parameters of this work simply acknowledge the need for investigation in this area and to be open to the possibility of alternative masculine embodiment.

Chamber has sought to offer deliberate and specific representations of masculinity but also attempts at times to sidestep representational forms altogether. It is as if within the constructed framework of *Chamber* there is another way, an anti-structure, which spills over into the rest of the work. This 'other way' is based on the use of improvised dancing over which I, as choreographer, have much less control. The improvisations are cracks in the surface of masculinity, which release something unexpected and unintentional, without the inherent contradictions being resolved.

The work Lloyd Newson and Steve Paxton have produced, and the ways they think about dance can be seen as two opposing referents in a spectrum. This spectrum runs from the representational (being like) to the non-representational (being) and acts to situate the choreographic and philosophical aims of *Chamber*. This dance spectrum can then be aligned to conflicts between masculine and feminine, mind and body, culture and nature – dualities that are all implicated in how the two choreographers address their work. Newson and Paxton have been involved, albeit in different ways, in challenging the manifestations of patriarchal control. While almost diametrically opposed in how they view dance, aspects of both choreographers' philosophies have been incorporated into *Chamber*. By examining aspects of their work I have aimed to illuminate the field of view within which *Chamber* teeters, falls and re-emerges.

CHAPTER THREE
THE PROCESS OF MAKING CHAMBER

Introduction – Key aims in the making of *Chamber*
There were several important agendas at play in the making of *Chamber*, often resulting in contradictory or conflictive outcomes. The primary drive behind the process was to make the piece centrally concerned with the problematic nature of masculinity. Far from the widely held view that masculinity is a straightforward proposition for men, the metaphorical impetus for the work is that men often live their lives at odds with the iconic symbols, behavioural patterns and bodily experiences of hegemonic masculinity. I was less concerned with presenting specific, socially situated problems which men might encounter in their daily lives, than with creating an exacting and complicated environment for the men to exist within. In so doing my intention was to metaphorically signal my belief that stereotypical masculinity needs to be confronted and questioned.

Another primary consideration was a desire to give form to the experiential dimension of men's lives, to the particularities of their 'lived' aspect, and to align this dimension clearly and strongly with the dancing body. Masculine experiences needed to be configured corporeally but also to be subjective and personal rather than universal or all encompassing; not the banner of uniformity under which all men can gather.

The icon or ideal of masculinity creates a situation of inadequacy for many men as they attempt to live up to the demands of the image but fail to do so. It was this contradiction I was also intent on capturing in the structure of *Chamber*. The aim was to contain something slippery and difficult to define within a fixed and, by association, 'masculine' structure as a metaphorical exploration of this contradiction. Consequently, *Chamber* was framed as a 'structured improvisation' in which the order of events was set and known but the movement material within each event (while operating within certain parameters) was changeable and indeterminate. The improvisation is reflective of the men's search for a subjective dimension and an alternative sense of identity. The difficulties in moving spontaneously without prior definition or certainty are representative of the struggle for masculine identity (something I shall expand upon later in this chapter). Within each man lies another realm of possibility, despite the fixed, stable image they might present to the world. It is a gesture toward an alternative space inside a familiar one, in which another, less known kind of dancing might emerge. This is the image of the chamber.

By associating masculinity with dancing I hoped to challenge the acceptable patterns of embodiment for men but also to expand the range of movement qualities commonly used in mainstream representations of the male dancer. The movement need not only be athletic and strong (or perhaps phallocentric if these qualities are over emphasized) but also soft, delicate, quiet, complicated, uncertain, neurotic, abject and any other number of qualities that might be regarded as rare for male dancing.

In response to these considerations I chose to work with three male dancers whom I felt would be prepared to invest emotionally, physically, intellectually and creatively in the process.[11]

---

[11] This was an obvious and straightforward choice under the circumstances but in practice it proved extremely difficult to find three male dancers appropriate to the challenge. To begin with there are far fewer male than female dancers. The male dancers also needed to be reasonably mature so as to draw on a depth of experience as well as feeling confident about exposing aspects of personal experience. Finally, the process was long and slow, requiring commitment and patience. The rewards for the dancers were in the creative extension the process offered and in the chance to develop a very personal engagement with movement and performance.

Their contributions made it possible for this work to hinge on a subjective engagement with the creative parameters and for this concentration to be maintained in performance.

Improvisation in *Chamber*
General approach
If one accepts that alternatives to hegemonic masculinity still lack definition or acknowledgement, the process for this work needed to be appropriately exploratory. How then could I tease out what the issues might be for these three dancers and myself in a way that privileged personal experience? How could aspects of our experience be translated into a movement form that is alive with distinctiveness and peculiarity? My response to this line of questioning was to focus on improvisation as both a working method and a performance medium. Although there are quite specifically set images in *Chamber*, the large majority of the work is improvised. The rational for this is not simply because of my personal experience of and partiality for the form. Improvisation also allows for the dynamics, movement preferences, spatial understanding and other manifestations of the embodied subjectivity of each dancer to be expressed in a relatively unfettered way [De Spain, 1995]. In an unstructured, open-ended improvisation the need for a choreographer would seem to be obsolete[12]. Yet even in a structured improvisation such as *Chamber*, the movement style and preferences of the choreographer are de-emphasized and control over what the dancers do is partially relinquished. This strategy seemed essential to a project which was endeavouring to unravel the intricacies of individual masculine experiences.

As a result of this strategy the movement material became extremely particular to those who danced it. Although I maintained a large degree of navigational control regarding the direction and form the piece would take, in many ways this piece was specifically *about* the experiences of the three dancers Simon Ellis, Martin Kwasner and Jacob Lehrer. *Chamber* was particular to their anatomical structure, to their kinaesthetic relationship to time and space, to their body image, and their unique interweaving of the psychical and the physical. Their motivation to move was determined by an internal or subjective source. This motivation was on occasion affected by my input or direction, but was also determined by their own responses to tasks over which I had limited control.

> *The practice of inward focusing, central to ideokinesis, places a person directly in touch with their own unique world of images, and with the unique operation of their own creative process. Spontaneous images, often filled with personal significance, are the very stuff of creativity, and exist as rich sources for dance. The ideokinetic method outlines a clear practice of incorporation, articulation and physicalization of images from image → action. In practice however the work more often than not moves in two directions, image ←→ action, image and movement constantly informing and modifying one another.* [Dempster, 1985 #61, p 20]

Dempster's passage provides a useful comparison. While the process employed in *Chamber* was not consciously based on ideokinesis,[13] the concerns and methods of ideokinesis run parallel to those of improvisation and indeed often overlap. Improvisation has the potential to draw upon the emotional, psychological and cultural positions of the dancer in extremely

---

[12] The dancers who are improvising in this open-ended fashion are determining the choreography in the moment of its actualization and thus can be credited with the outcome in the same way a singular and premeditated choreographic intention might be.
[13] Ideokinesis is the process of experiencing or generating movement in response to an idea, an image or a sensation which is usually based on anatomical information.

complicated ways, ways which are often more difficult to verbally articulate than physically express. There is often a kind of 'universe of possibilities' within improvisation but despite this, very personal, intimate moments emerge that speak strongly about the ways that individual engages with the world. The dancer's physical disclosures are imbued with the personal, acting as a conduit between the internal machinations of consciousness and the audience's scrutiny of the object body. These disclosures inevitably reflect his understanding about how his private self meets the world.

The dancer's culturally attuned aspect will also inevitably be exhibited in his improvising as surely as a man walks, sits, throws and runs differently from a woman. Men's bodies carry clear gender codification as strongly as women's bodies do. Sally Gardner, in talking about the post-modern dance practices of certain 1960s and 1970s choreographers, says that "By placing necessarily coded bodies in non-representational or 'other' contexts they contributed to a displacement or unsettling of conventional readings of the body" [Gardner, 1996 #45, p 56]. I would argue that improvisation offers this occasion for disruption, for surprise, for revealing what was not known, for disturbing the habitual. This is when the veneer of masculinity may slip for a moment. This is when the dancer's fixed gaze is interrupted to reveal pleasure or fear; when his body becomes animated by the fleeting, long-forgotten memory; when he forgets himself and moves with a delicacy and fluidity he may never have achieved when dancing in predetermined choreography. This immersion in the moment of improvisation has the capacity to suspend the requirements of the masculine order. Gardner continues by saying:

> Earlier, I suggested that the idea of 'neutrality' in certain dance practices might also be formulated in terms of their aiming to make the body available for re-inscription in 'other' ways. These practices require a certain ambience or environment – a space and time in which purposes and activities are strategically suspended, perhaps to enable the dance to move 'in a space emptied of things and thus of the order of things' as Alphonso Lingis suggests – space for a wilful hesitation during which a gap might be opened for the creation of a different kind of bodily order. [Gardner, 1996 #45, p 55]

This was the spirit in which *Chamber* was investigated. The outcomes in performance still exhibit strong links to the old order and the inherent contradictions it contains. But the project was an attempt by us as men to engage with this ideal and to initiate a small and particular re-embodiment of masculinity.

The rehearsal process was explored within a certain framework; feeling was privileged and discussion of the outcomes valued. No attempt was made to impose a shape or template on the process; rather the shape emerged from the process. The rehearsal period was underpinned by an intuitive response to the development and formation of the final performance. By improvising the material, by drawing on the personal resources of each dancer and by working on tasks which emphasized neutrality over specific gender representation, we aimed to avoid a logocentric or instrumentalist approach and so not directly reinforce the dualities of mind and body or masculine and feminine. Many of the tasks that emphasized neutrality were based on the use of touch to stimulate sensation, memory and association in the dancers. They were then open to interpret this information in a context free from external points of reference, focusing on the movement responses the information elicited (I shall expand on this work with touch later in this chapter).

Uses of improvisation in process and performance
There were three distinct methods in which improvisation was employed. The first of these was as a way to play with an idea or an image I had previously devised and consequently where the intention was predetermined. These ideas seemed necessary, despite my intention of being open to the discovery of material through the improvisational process, in order to anchor the piece in the context I had set out for myself. These ideas would then be interpreted as scores for the dancers to improvise with and the results either further developed or discarded. The outcomes would then be loosely 'set'. For example, the image of Simon and Martin walking toward the audience with pants down and shirts up was constructed in this way. This image began with the idea for the text (an authoritative voice reading the executive employment advertisements) and was originally constructed as something more physically complex. But as the dancers played with the instructions (involving a degree of set movement and them sitting on chairs) I began to whittle down the movement content until we were left with the simple act of walking in a straight line toward the audience.

Another use for improvisation was as a method for exploration when I had only a very vague definition of what the possibilities might be. I would ask the dancers to improvise around a loose score without the expectation that I might use this score in its current state. For example when I asked the dancers to dance cheek to cheek, this was the limit of the instruction. In my mind there was a question about what effect might emerge from three men dancing in such an intimate relationship. What they did with this instruction was completely open, at least initially, and refined in its intention as we rehearsed it. This method was essentially a way of scanning for material but without knowing what I wanted or hoped to find. Often this was a way of investigating a specific context in which to view the movement ideas.

Sometimes instruction was completely abandoned in the course of an improvisation and new material was discovered which was exciting and had the dancers completely absorbed. The decision about the appropriateness of this material (did it fit into the work?) was suspended as I attempted to follow an intuitive response to the material and defer judgement about how the work would crystallize. If the outcome of an improvisation was fresh and engaging we would work with it until a later time when a more formal editing and structuring process occurred.

Finally, improvisation was used as a performance mode in its own right. That is to say the movement material was discovered for the first time in performance with no relationship to anything done in rehearsal. Usually there were elements of structure containing these improvisations but no predetermined score. The main examples of this in *Chamber* were when touch was used as motivation for the dancers' movement. The quality of the touch and the dancer's response to it determined the nature of the movement material. This was an element over which I had very little or even no control. The structure that inhibited the dancers to a degree in these sections was the consideration about where in the space they danced (so as to effectively light their actions in the space or to provide room for another event to occur) and to a certain extent how long they danced for.[14] Outside of this they were free to find fresh material in each performance. This ploy was at the heart of my desire to keep the piece alive, risky and indeterminate and for it to be embedded in the personal signatures of the men dancing in it.

---

[14] My standard instruction in response to the length of these improvisations would be to encourage them to spend longer in the state and to spend time searching for fresh material each night.

Effects of improvisation on my role as choreographer
As a choreographic tool then, improvisation can reverberate with the sentience of the male dancers themselves. It also allowed for the unexpected in what I, as a male choreographer, see as possible. Improvisation interrupted the habitual in my choreographic sensibility, letting me work in an intuitive way rather than following a blueprint of choreographic intent. This enabled me to engage in a process of trial and error, of feeling my way, of touching the contours of the thing before it is seen.

My role as choreographer shifted between two models. The first model was that of the traditional choreographer who was directly responsible for the material and transcribed this unchanged onto the dancers (although the occasions that this occurred were extremely rare).[15] The second model was the dominant one, in which I played a more directorial role, less physically involved but shaping and structuring the contributions of the dancers themselves. Their work altered in response to my thoughts or suggestions but the actualisation of these thoughts, was carried out by the dancers themselves. This model was used for the bulk of the material generated and kept for the final form of the work.

None of this diminishes my impact on the work. My sensibility was evident throughout in the choice of movement instructions (scores), in the chronological placement of sections, in the juxtaposition and combination of discrete movement sections and images, or in the collaborations I had with the composer and video makers. I was alone in having access to and an understanding of all of the elements that went into the making of *Chamber*. My choice of a very specific strategy of cultivating the indeterminate in the choreographic process and shaping the structures this entailed gave the piece its tenor and defining qualities. However, the contributions of the dancers (and the other artists involved) gave the work a greater depth and level of intimacy: a deeper well of experiences from which to draw.

The rehearsal process
General approach
Rehearsals for *Chamber* were conducted over approximately two years. Large periods of time within this period were left dormant due to other commitments of the dancers involved. These down times would often last up to three months.[16] When rehearsals were regularly conducted we generally met once a week. The exceptions to this were when the performances drew closer, with several rehearsals a week being scheduled for up to three weeks. The slow development process was both frustrating and rewarding. The difficulties encountered by rehearsing so infrequently certainly created a lack of momentum for the project on several occasions. However, the gaps between rehearsals left me plenty of time to think about the direction of the work and to sit with ideas without the pressure of an immediate decision. In this sense the work was able to have a long gestation period which I believe significantly aided in its development. It also enabled the compilation of ideas and references which were defined and collected slowly, and from disparate sources. I stumbled across information about the treatment of disease in plants from an old gardening book and intuitively made a connection to the work in a way I feel would have been difficult had I been on a more pressured timeline.

In fact the open-ended nature of the project required me to create deadlines for myself within this time frame, so as to accelerate the process toward a specific goal. These goals were a

---

[15] The image of Martin and Simon walking toward the audience with shirts lifted and trousers down was a section which I initially introduced in this way.
[16] One of the principle difficulties in working on this project was in fact finding common rehearsal time for all involved. The choice to work with mature and experienced dancers meant they were also less available to me. However, another consequence of their maturity was that they were able to engage in a dialogue about the process and their involvement in it.

work-in-progress showing at Cecil St Studio in Fitzroy, Melbourne, on May 4 2001 and a fully produced and publicly advertised performance over two nights at Dancehouse, North Carlton, Melbourne, on July 7-8 2001. The work-in-progress showing was to an invited audience who were asked to offer responses and feedback to the sections of dancing which were shown. The offering at that stage was an unfinished series of sections, grouped together in an order for the occasion but with no apparent links to each other. While the Dancehouse performances were of a completed work, it also acted as a way of testing the viability of the choreography.

These public showings enabled me to see how an audience would influence the improvisation capacities and preferences of the dancers, which in turn indicated (more clearly than in a rehearsal situation) their strengths and weaknesses. An audience also seems to create a more objective situation from which to view the work. It was as if I was able to see it with a new eye, suddenly acutely aware of the implications of the dancing as if unveiled by the audience response. I was then able to work toward the final performances from the luxurious position of sensing how it would work in performance and knowing what I was unhappy with. Several sections were altered and fine-tuned and an extended ending added as a result of the Dancehouse performances.[17]

The development of some key rehearsal scores
The touch improvisations
Many early rehearsals and improvisations centred on using touch as an entry point to an improvisation. With eyes closed, one dancer received the tactile information given by a partner. This was not the alignment-specific touching \ many dancers are so familiar with, but qualities of touch that were erratic, delicate, flippant, annoying or unexpected. When the touching finished, the dancer used the physical memory of the experience as source material for their improvisation. The results in movement were often imbued with a sense of rich association to memories and personal experience no verbal instruction could hope to achieve. These dances were very personal in the ways they played out, and riveting to watch because of the dancer's attention to the quality of the experience.

The touch improvisations proved to be an exceptionally rich resource and one that created different responses each time we did it. The tactile information was easy to vary and extremely changeable in the kinds of responses it generated. Assimilation of the information received from these tactile sessions often proved to be extremely complex. It was difficult to capture a particular thought or association: sometimes memories would be brought to life, sometimes feelings, sometimes sensations which felt familiar or alternatively quite strange. We deliberately avoided the kind of tactile work dancers often experience in release-based dance classes. We did not, for example, use specific patterns of touch which were designed to increase awareness of particular postural or alignment goals, such as might be used in a Skinner Release Technique class. The aim was not to make the dancers move more efficiently but to stimulate a personal response. As such, the touch was often erratic and random or with variable qualities of pressure.

Several sections of *Chamber* drew on the work developed in these sessions. Jacob's second solo, performed on the elevated section at the back of the space, is a response to the tactile contact of Martin and Simon. Simon's solo downstage is a response to the larger, full-bodied manipulations Jacob performs on him. And Jacob is again the tactile protagonist to Martin's soloing during and directly after Simon's solo. In their physical interpretations, all of the

---

[17] The ending was significantly altered and extended after the 2001 Dancehouse performances. I also changed in subtle ways the two men walking forward with trousers down and the relationship of Simon's solo after Jacob's touch to Martin's presence upstage.

35

dancers were attempting to remain as true as possible to the reception, memory and associations of these complex stimuli.

As we watched in rehearsals the act of one person giving the tactile information and another receiving it, it seemed to me that this was in fact a duet. There was just as much interest for me in watching what kind of approach the toucher would take as there was in watching the improvisation that ensued. This then developed into a score where Martin and Simon used wooden sticks to touch Jacob to see if there was a noticeable difference. The metaphor I was interested in concerned a more clinical form of touch, where the warmth and support of touch could be held at bay. A more objectified, medical or scientific kind of touching might speak more about the difficulties men have in touching each other free of any sexual overtones. But in the reworking of this idea we discarded the sticks as an unnecessary and clumsy addition. Martin and Simon were able to apply a kind of 'measuring and testing' form of touch without them. This created a slightly mysterious extension of Jacob's personally absorbed solo at the very opening of the piece.

The secrets improvisations
Score: think of a secret you have never told anyone and use your feelings, thoughts and associations of this memory to initiate movement.

This score was given to each dancer separately and at different rehearsals. They spent some time thinking about a situation from their own lives which they had never revealed to anyone else as the basis for their improvisation. My intention was to work in an area of some discomfort for the dancers and to site this discomfort in their own experience. I did not discover what the secrets were for any of the three dancers. The interest for me lay not with the content of their 'secrets' but in how they responded to them in movement.

The outcome of this exploration for Martin was a knotty and troubled solo in which he buries his head in the crook of his elbow and struggles with his own insubordinate hand. For Simon there is an equally edgy motif of thrashing arm and deep squats combined with moments of him quietly speaking ('there was blood... the first time. How do you tell someone?'). With Jacob the situation was slightly different: he claimed not to have a secret that he never told anyone. Instead, he said, all his secrets were told to various people in different ways. What developed out of his response was an improvisation where he began telling a story about Simon – a completely fabricated scenario – Simon felt inclined to put a stop to by putting his hand over Jacob's mouth. By working with this beginning the scene was rearranged slightly to have Simon begin to tell a story and for Jacob to stop him and then for Jacob to take over by telling a story about Simon. Jacob told a different story for most performances and managed to keep the surprise and expectation for Simon quite genuine.

The challenge, in the development of these three fragments of material, was to re-find the same state of feeling and quality of movement. This was material which I felt warranted being presented with its original intensity, rather than providing a space for more open-ended improvisation. They also provided strong references to the nature of the struggle for identity these men were engaged in.

Goya improvisations
The so-called Goya improvisations were sessions that used as impetus the grotesque, black and white prints of 19th century Spanish artist Francisco Goya. More specifically we drew on the series of prints loosely entitled *Los Disparates*.

These prints contain more or less absurd, Surrealistic images: bulls flying through the air, an elephant staring motionless at a group of men, people crouching like frozen birds on a branch, a horse catapulting a woman into the air, distorted faces screaming silently, and people fleeing from phantom. The Disparates could be described as a series of dreams. For just like nocturnal dreams they are strange and familiar. Whoever tries to decipher them is groping in the dark. This enigmatic quality is precisely what endows the series with modernity. These subjects are no longer drawn from the traditional language of artistic images, but from a private world. [Buchholz, 1999: 80]

It was this enigmatic quality I was drawn to and the metaphor is quite straightforward. Masculinity, groping in the dark, uncertain of its own interpretation, and surprised and frightened by what steps out from the shadows. The sense of the grotesque in the prints, which I equated with a fear of the unknown, linked closely with my intentions for *Chamber*. The ambiguity was also attractive; no clear answers, no easy options and a search for meaning.

These prints generated responses which formed the latter part of *Chamber*. The duet between Martin and Simon was conceived as an embodiment of two of the characters from the print entitled *Disparate Carnaval* (*Carnaval Folly*) [Heckes, 1998: 74].

By beginning in the pose and attitude of these two strange figures Simon and Martin slowly fleshed out, over numerous attempts, a duet which for me captured the spirit of these figures. Jacob's slightly comical character who makes a surprising entrance after this duet was also a progeny of these prints. His print was called *Disparate de bobo* (*Simpleton*) [Heckes, 1998: 75] and features a huge simpleton with a broad but eerie grimace [Buchholz, 1999: 81]. Jacob slipped into a kind of approximation of this character quite readily, but his introduction created a huge shift in focus for the performance as a whole. I was not able to resolve this shift to my satisfaction, despite feeling like the introduction of this darkly amusing dullard was entirely fitting.

Video and sound in Chamber
Video
By adding video footage to Chamber my intention was to give the performance another texture and another layer so as to complicate the environment even further. By doing this, the metaphor of masculinity grappling with a problem would be heightened. And coming at the same issue from different perspectives – live performance and video – the 'problem' could be contemplated from various angles. The screen image seems to me to have a special kind of authority, one that seems to be more pervasive and easily understood than live performance, even if the video image is of dance. Close-ups with the camera also suggest intimacy, something I felt screen-saturated audiences could instantly recognize. The close-up was important as a way to suggest introspection, such as the section which focuses in fine detail on Jacob's face and hands. But this reflexivity is thrown into turmoil by the video editing techniques, cutting quickly between images and incorporating swirling, abstract collages of colour.

The men were also seen in different, often very dramatic environments such as the University of Melbourne underground car park. This allowed me to create a sense of three-dimensional, bricks-and-mortar enclosure in way that would have required much more elaborate staging if attempted in a live performance setting. Other images show trees and blue sky giving a glimpse of an outside space with an accompanying sense of escape or openness, even if this is quickly subverted.

Sound

The sound score was like the glue that held the work together. Often quite subtle and understated it nevertheless creates an acute sense of the environment in which the men exist. It offers an atmospheric intensity which was crucial in drawing together, the often-disparate choreographic and improvised material in *Chamber*. David Corbet performed some sections of the soundscore live, such as the harmonium accompanying the cheek-to-cheek trio. Or he manipulated and mixed computer-based sound bites in real time, often in different ways in different performances, to match or complement the differences the dancers experienced within improvised scores.

The sound also bolstered the metaphorical intent of certain sections by way of pre-recorded text or the choice of sounds to dramatically frame the dancing. The 'Goya' duet between Simon and Martin is accompanied by a harsh, piercing mix of sounds that build into a tearing crescendo before fading away. The sound suggests the tension that is reflected in the faces and bodies of the dancers. I was always clear that there should be very no harmonically composed 'music' in *Chamber*, so as to avoid diluting the specific ambience of the 'chamber'. Musical familiarity would have offered a 'way out' for audiences which would have made the work more comfortable, but less uncompromising.

Conclusion

By using improvisation as a tool and by focusing on the dancing subjectivities of the men involved I aimed to relate the process of making *Chamber* to the theoretical issues outlined earlier in this work. The investigation orbited around problems associated with a hegemonic formulation of masculinity whereby I attempted to create a complex performance environment that would resist the seeming simplicity that hegemonic masculinity demands. Extending from this theme was the desire to associate men with the body. More specifically, this required an avoidance of 'universalism' by privileging the individual dancing subjectivities of the male dancers involved. Their improvised and embodied specificities, manifest in their movement, were built into the very structure of the piece. Indeed the piece was structured so as to contain them.

But it was not my intention to ignore the power of hegemonic masculinity. *Chamber* swings between references to this power and the desire to open another space for possibility. Representation and non-representation in dance both uncomfortably co-exist in the work, intermingling at times, and at other points necessarily separate, anxious about the other's presence and uncertain of any equilibrium. The shifting ground represents a challenge to the exclusive authority of representation and closure as markers of hegemonic values. These approaches to making the dance functioned as strategies for investigating to what extent I could subvert hegemonic constructions of the dancing male.

CHAPTER FOUR
LOOKING INTO THE CHAMBER

Introduction
What follows in this chapter is a full and detailed account of *Chamber* from my perspective as the choreographer, so as to make clear my intentions for each section of the work. Consequently, choreographic intention can be located in relation to the range of objective viewpoints from which one might interpret the work. However, *Chamber* is a structured improvisation and accordingly the movement content and the quality of it changed (to a greater or lesser degree depending on the section) with each performance. Because of this, what I describe in this chapter is something of an amalgam of my time spent watching repeated rehearsals and performances. There may be minor or even significant variations between what I describe here and how another viewer might interpret or receive *Chamber*, variations that go beyond the usual variance of interpretation of a dance work.

Choreographer's Description of *Chamber*
Chamber opens with Jacob sensitively lit at the back of the space, framed by black but distanced further by the veil of sheer black cotton. Self-absorbed and with eyes closed, he reaches upward, outward, with no urgency, calmly gesturing and shifting weight. His focus is internal, an indication or metaphor for the self-reflection that motivates his measured movement; his fingers, hands and arms articulating the 'searching' he is engaged in. This is not an image of masculinity uncomfortable with itself. This is a man able to 'look inside', to enter the chamber of the male psyche. The sound is of subterranean water with the associative qualities of contained fluidity and depth. Yet this is not an immediate or forthright image of masculinity. His self-absorption is delicate, never direct or bold. The man seems elusive or slippery, unwilling to conform but unable to present himself fully.

Simon and Martin enter from either side of the narrow frame of light. They place Jacob's hands on his head, a position of submission, and begin to poke, slice, prod, test and measure the surface of his body. They maintain a slightly clinical air, at times testing and then observing with a 'scientific' regard for the subject and his physicality (the body is an instrument). Simon and Martin are not so overt as to tip the event into farce or gothic melodrama. And there is a mystery about the whole procedure as if those without the knowledge or training – the uninitiated – could never understand the full implications of what was being done to Jacob.

But this procedure also has a strategic function. Jacob, in receiving this tactile information, is formulating a physical response. His solo, after the others leave, is a direct manifestation of his associative response to the touch he receives. This response is changeable, but often manifests in sharp, jerky cuts of his elbows and knees and a pushing out from the axial body as if trying to expel something. His sense of calm and self-assurance has dissolved in the face of his interaction with order, logic, power and the men who wield it.

The scene shifts. A sudden beam of light captures Martin and Simon sitting with hands behind their backs, pants dropped around their ankles and chests bared. The accompanying voice-over delivers executive job descriptions with an authoritative, and at times menacing, tone. The position descriptions, taken from the Saturday newspaper's Executive Employment section, detail the skills and attributes needed to succeed as a high-powered business executive. The language is harsh, the requirements of the jobs impressive and the combined impact of the overlay of these advertisements metaphorically overwhelming. The two men begin to walk toward the audience, their bare skin reflecting their vulnerability in the face of this aural assault but their faces unable to register any emotion. They look defeated.

The piece segues into a video solo of Jacob. He is filmed at times in extreme close up emphasizing a sense of intimacy. This is a return to the reflective figure the piece opens with. But the video footage is also blurry on occasion and cuts between shots erratically so a consistent viewing is difficult. The subjectivity of this man is highlighted but simultaneously difficult to grasp.

As the video image fades the three men stride into the space. They walk and turn, aware of each other's presence but tentative because of this. They begin to edge toward one another, then breaking away to return to a walk. The skittishness fades as they reach towards each other, finally offering a cheek to connect with another's. They relax as the three of them connect cheek to cheek, a single moving entity. Their breathing softens as they release into the sensuality and kinaesthetic of the 'score'. They drop to the floor always seeking to stay connected cheek to cheek, but physical necessity sometimes determines that they separate. Quickly they return to the point of connection. The quality is gentle, tender even, despite the physical manoeuvring that the score requires. The harmonium provides a warm backdrop to this supportive and cooperative image. Despite the faltering start, they embody intimacy or trust in their connection.

This stands out as one of the few moments of ease and warmth in what transpires to be an increasingly bleak and claustrophobic journey. The chamber is not an easy place to be in. The discomfort and struggle alludes to the difficulties men encounter in 'climbing the ramparts' of hegemonic masculinity, but also of realizing the possibility of opposition to this monolith. It is not easy. It is problematic.

As the cheek-to-cheek trio runs its course, Martin finds himself excluded and leaves. The focus dissolves as a spotlight isolates Simon and Jacob, standing facing the audience. Simon exhales as if expelling any vestige of the previous event. He then begins to speak to the audience as if telling them a personal story. His story sounds plausibly idiosyncratic – "when I was young I was really small and my brother, who was seven years older than me, used to call me snagglegrass…" He is cut off in mid sentence as Jacob covers his mouth with his hand. Jacob removes his hand to let Simon continue only to repeat the disruption. It is a boyish moment, playful and silly. But Jacob then replaces Simon as the one telling his 'story' to the audience (again, his complicity with the audience seems genuine, but is not, his story changing if not each night, then gradually over several performances). As Jacob speaks Simon covers his mouth, attempting to silence him. As the act is repeated Simon's concern increases and he becomes more determined. The game teeters towards something more aggressive, more muscular. They begin to wrangle and when Jacob again puts his hand on Simon's mouth they are locked in a kind of mutual clamp. The underlying soundscape that has been simmering underneath begins to intensify to a menacing throb. The game has disintegrated into something more dangerous and adult. Any sense of 'mateship' has been disturbed by an uncertainty about the unfinished 'stories' and the surge of aggression. They finally peel their hands away in stalemate.

The piece returns to an earlier strategy for generating improvised dance material. Simon closes his eyes and Jacob begins to carve Simon's skin with the edge of his hand. Jacob lifts and drops Simon's arm, or lifts his whole body weight on his knee. He pokes, slices, brushes, digs and scratches Simon's surface. It looks as if to be a bizarre continuation of the previous duel, and in a sense it is. But it is also a leap into another kind of logic. Then Jacob leaves indicating the beginning of Simon's solo. This is Simon 'embodying' his subjectivity, his identity, and his memory as Jacob's touch triggers a plethora of complex images and sensations, and plunges him into a rich realm of association. There is immediacy about his response that never seems to diminish with the repetition in performance. It is hard to get used to this. The touching asks many questions and Simon is impelled to give account; his responses are telling without any words to describe them. He encounters many divergent narratives in this act, jumbled and confused, but always embodied. There is an existential dimension to Simon's ensuing solo that the audience can kinaesthetically sense but never quite see.

The intense, almost ritual quality is made more complex by the appearance of Martin in the upstage corner. Martin progresses on a diagonal towards Simon stopping three times. At each pause he performs small solos that are twitchy, staccato, erratic little cameos – minute collapses of identity. He seems drawn to Simon as if Simon has an understanding of something, which he lacks – perhaps a psychological clarity regarding the ailment he suffers. But Simon, unaware of his presence, offers nothing. Martin backs away to re-engage with his own uncertainties, reconfiguring his body in sharp breaks at the hips and bursts of tensile movement. He cannot find a comfortable and sustained rhythm.

Jacob re-enters and walks over to Martin. He catches him by the shoulders and stills Martin's disorder. Martin pauses, averts his eyes, unable to grasp any possibility of comfort from Jacob's actions. The scene is repeated three times. Each time Jacob releases him, Martin returns to his malaise like an addiction, unable or unwilling to take comfort from the physical contact. Jacob leaves. He has nothing more to offer.

The focus again switches to the video screens on either side of the space. The three men are filmed in a long corridor space with pillars demarcating a 'chamber' for each of them. The video is densely edited with complicated overlays of image and movement. One of the men moves then disappears to be replaced seamlessly by one of the others. A shadowy image of Martin appears, sits in repose and watches himself dancing. The blurring trail of movement left by Simon is somewhat reminiscent of the smudged and anguished paintings of Francis Bacon.

The videos intensify the focus on the three men. The screen image seems able to provide a powerful authority to their struggles. But these images also provide a change of texture and pace from the dark intensity maintained in the live performance.

Throughout the work this intensity is developed and bolstered by the nature of the soundscape. The low hums and throbs, the persistent ticks and ambient water sounds are what connect the various sections to each other, particularly live performance to video. The sound is sometimes barely noticeable; instead it is more felt as aural immersion, swimming around the dancers and giving the piece viscosity. Against this we feel the warmth of the harmonium (played live) like sunshine on a cold day.

As the video ends Martin, Jacob and Simon walk forward and address the audience. They state their names and a few personal details. They all talk at once and the information is garbled, but we discover enough to know that these are brief biographies. This is who they are; they have identified themselves. And yet as they finish talking and retreat away from the audience they seem less sure of themselves. Perhaps identity is not so secure.

Their uncertainty gives way to cleaning, scratching and obsessing as the voice-over narration begins. The narrator details the effects of various diseases on plants and how best to purge them with the use of powerful chemicals. The associative link between a gardening treatise and masculinity is a tenuous one. Yet by association the men are being compared to organisms that carry disease, and the tone of the narrator indicates such organisms must be eradicated. The three men dance alone and then together as three simultaneous solos. They are variously fluid, erratic, reflective, powerful. But the juxtaposition with the narration is unsettling and the effect is insidious; it undermines the authority of the three men and any straightforward pleasure we (the audience) might have in watching their obvious skill with movement.

The return to the video offers some relief. Birds sing and we see images of a blue sky through a window. There is light outside the chamber. The video continues with the natural imagery – flowers, trees, then houses and more trees. But the tranquillity is disturbed. The image spins and whirls breaking into an abstraction of colour and texture. The accompanying sound becomes shrill and eerie and the colours bleed out to black and white. As the swirl decelerates we are again surrounded by the hue of cut stone; we are again inside a built environment, a room, a chamber, a prison.

This is emphasized by a claustrophobic compression of space and time that sets in as the three men return to the space. We now sense that their room has a very low ceiling. The ceiling has become very low and they seem unable to find new purpose or renewal. The mood is grim but poised.

As they return to pacing the room, Jacob coils, hardens and then explodes in a fit of rage and frustration. There is a sense of Jacob acting as a kind of protagonist in the relationships between the three men. Martin and Simon often seem more ready to comply with the demands stereotypical masculinity makes of their identity. Their inability to see beyond this framework is reflected in Jacob's rage. Simon and Martin freeze, incapacitated by Jacob's plea, dumb in response. Jacob picks himself up and begins a dance heavy with apathy. Martin echoes his movements in as shadowy duet as a way to offer solace or support, but he is not up to the task. The task overwhelms him, and as the two men sit on the floor, Martin gets caught in a tangle of frantic gesturing with his arms and hands. Jacob leaves the space.

The focus shifts to Simon upstage, caught in a shaft of light. His solo combines sharp pumps of his right arm, wiping gestures to his mouth and anus and snippets of dialogue ("there was blood…" – "the first time…" – "how do you tell someone?"). There is no clarity about what he is referring to but it hints at sexual misadventure and menace, the agitation in his movements serving to heighten the tension. We cannot fill in the gaps but are left to ponder his situation and witness his personal struggle.

Martin then begins a solo in the same vein but the metaphor is more actualised in movement. Barely visible in the dim light, he rolls from his sitting position onto his left elbow and lifts his hips while he tucks his head into the angle of his elbow. His left hand seems to have no relationship to the rest of his body; it is beyond his conscious control. He tries to keep it still with his other hand but it flops uncontrollably like a wayward fish. His struggle continues as he comes to standing and wrestles with himself, his head chafing against his outstretched arm. His struggle to 'control' his body is evocative of the 'masculine' need to control, to regiment or to order. His will seems in conflict with his body as he fights to tame this unexpected bodily agency.

Finally Martin releases from the struggle and sensing Simon's presence on the other side of the space walks slowly towards him. They stand face to face as if confronting each other, or perhaps facing themselves in some sort of projected mirror image. But as they face each other the video emerges again. The three men appear in an underground space. The space is dramatic in design with arches and columns, vaulted like a catacomb. The video is erratic, mad and chaotic. It cuts between images quickly or blurs, but we are able to see the men caught in moments of disarray in their movement. The images are unsettling, even frightening. They are trapped.

The duet that builds between Simon and Martin tips the work into a realm beyond rationality. Slowly as their faces tense and their centres of gravity drop, they metamorphose into something edging on the grotesque. Their faces distort as their bodies interweave and pull apart. The constant assaults on their sense of identity seem finally to have stripped them of any veneer of normality or easy masculinity. Here masculinity is in complete disarray, without comfortable points of reference whereby they could be classified as strong or bold or virile or even handsome. Instead masculinity has been cut adrift in an unfamiliar expanse.

Jacob's entrance has the potential for comic relief as he mugs like a simpleton and meanders around the space, humming quietly to himself. But the laugh is still a black one as he too has lost any resemblance to temperate masculinity. He has become a deranged and gormless caricature as he skips and frolics through the shadowy light. His is a contradictory presence – funny and bleak, a simpleton but complex in his impact, unskilled a dancer in a way that takes great skill. He can negotiate the uncertainty of the place they have all arrived in, in a way the other two cannot, merely because he is beyond caring. But this ability marks him as even less of a man. He is stranger in the final analysis because he has stepped further over the line of demarcation that gives psychological definition to a man. As he sits down on Martin's supine form and blinks cheerily into the light, the poetry of James K. Baxter[18] casts an apocalyptic pall over the stillness [Baxter, 1982: 116].

As the poem continues Jacob picks up a groggy partner for a waltz (or a comparable partner dance). Martin flops and stumbles in a forlorn approximation, while Jacob seems oblivious to Martin's incapacitation. Jacob's intention is simple and narrow and completely dysfunctional and he is having a fine time. He discards Martin to leap and prance by himself in bacchanalian style before he exits the space. There is no straightforward reading to the image except to say that it is a picture of degraded masculinity; a masculinity that is being buffeted by a power it cannot seem to apprehend or control.

The final image in the work sees the three men dancing simultaneously, but each one alone in a pool of light. Simon's dancing expands and constricts as he alternates between dynamic, full-bodied movements and tight, neurotic hand gestures. Martin hobbles on the outside edges of his feet, his fingers hooked into his mouth or with his arm clutched between his thighs. With his slow, meditative searching with outstretched arms and sensitive hands, Jacob revives *Chamber*'s opening image.

No communication occurs. The sound score, characterized by a nervous, erratic ticking sound maintains the tightly held atmosphere. The suggestion is that although there are different outcomes for each man, they are still seemingly trapped on a treadmill. It is a sombre, even depressing ending, particularly as it lacks a redemptive aspect. In a way it does not feel like an

---

[18] See 'The Black Star' by New Zealand poet James K. Baxter

CHAPTER FIVE
REFLECTIONS ON CHAMBER

The development of the piece in performance

Chamber was performed in its final iteration over three evenings and two afternoons from 25 - 28 May 2002.[19] Performances were held in the intimate atmosphere of the Sylvia Staehli Theatre and were a brief but intensely satisfying reward for the long hours spent on their conception. One of the most satisfying aspects of watching the piece unfold in front of an audience was seeing how it took on a life of its own. The work seemed to expand and contract and take on an organic shape in ways I had not seen in rehearsals. The dancers, spurred on by the presence of an audience, came to life and injected fresh imaginative spirit into their movement. They also came to understand *Chamber* in a much more intimate way; in a way that only the experience of the work in performance seems to bring. This sharpened the dancers' sense of timing, heightened their awareness of their movement and of each other, and let them occupy the space with greater performance presence. There was no longer the necessity to 'think' their way through the performance, able instead to 'be' in the movement and to intuit the implications one moment or one gesture would have for the next. As a result *Chamber* changed in subtle but discernible ways over the course of the performance season. These shifts were never seismic or glaring, yet there was steady centrifugal pull toward focus – like watching a Polaroid photograph develop before your eyes until the image is sharply defined.

Watching *Chamber* with an audience present, watching material I had become so familiar with that I could no longer 'see it', also enabled me to be more objective about the work. I was able to release any responsibility for the actualisation of the material (relying on the skills and bearing of the dancers) and view it from a greater distance. On the whole this was both edifying and enjoyable but there were some facets of the piece that I came to see as problematic. In retrospect the primary problem in the reading of the piece was the ultimate denial of any hope for these three men. They were put through quite a degree of turmoil without respite. This was in fact intentional at the outset: that I should be uncompromising in my application of pressure. But in the end it seemed appropriate that they be released, at least at some point, from the intensity that encased them. When I relive this now, the ending in particular seems morbidly circular, condemning them to a repetitive existential void.

Structured improvisation

From the outset I pursued the agenda of complicating masculinity and of sullying the iconic uniformity it often still holds. I believe I succeeded in doing this but at a certain cost. It appears to me upon reflection that the 'alternative space in which men might dance', the kind of utopian aspiration which was also an initial desire, became overshadowed by the sheer weight of the reaction to hegemonic masculinity. It was a conflict in a piece about contradictions. And possibly the most tenuous proposition was that a structured improvisation was in fact possible. My response to this is that *Chamber* succeeded in presenting masculinity as problematic and in aligning men with embodiment. But the necessary desire to articulate this very context curtailed the possibility of the movement spontaneously shifting to another context or to another dynamic or to another realm of the unexpected. This degree of indeterminacy is what an unstructured improvisation can offer and while indeterminacy was present in *Chamber* it did not dominate. What came to dominate in the final analysis was the structure of the work – the elements that remained immutable from performance to performance. Because of this I think *Chamber* could be understood or interpreted from a more singular vantage point. But the more

---

[19] For program notes see appendix 1.

ephemeral and unexpected dancing moments that improvised dance can produce were less evident or distinct under the weight of the structure.

Renowned teacher Mary Fulkerson talks about a distinction; Ramsay Burt discusses this:

> ...between work that is 'trying to be like' something else and work that is just 'trying to be'. Although work that is 'trying to be like' can be pleasing through being familiar, it doesn't interest Fulkerson: 'It is work that tries "to be" which puzzles, angers, moves, challenges me and keeps my attention'. [Burt, 1995: 71]

It is the hinge between the realms that Fulkerson describes, between the 'trying to be like' and the 'being' on which *Chamber* teetered. *Chamber* does have symbolic structure. The order of events and images were thought about and decided upon, certain images were developed as direct representational references to masculinity, and the video imagery was incorporated as symbolic markers for the movement. In other words the context for the movement was deliberate and directly referential. But the movement was often not intentionally referential to the masculine order – even if it came to be seen that way by association. The structures were designed so that I would have limited control over the outcome and this was the offering to a possible alternative for masculine identity or construction. But despite this aim, my sense is that the movement was too fragile to rise above the rigidity of the structure. The context for *Chamber* was clear but the alternatives were never fully realized.

I do not wish to undermine the original spirit, the impact or the achievements of *Chamber*. I feel the performances had integrity and power in dealing with the issues in the way it did. I also learnt how to create choreography in, from my perspective, a new way. To have completely handed over responsibility for all of the movement to the dancers, and to have built their contributions into a coherent piece was a very different approach for me. The challenge was always about finding how to communicate my intentions and needs in a format that facilitated their movement exploration. I could not *show* them what I wanted. Indeed often I did not precisely *know* what I wanted. There was a substantial amount of trial and error and suspension of judgement about the appropriateness of rehearsal material – something that the dancers handled with good humour and sensitivity. Improvisation showed me how much greater the range of options were and how often the surprises in rehearsal were so much more powerful than any movement idea I might have presupposed. I afforded myself the 'space' to sit with ideas, and work them through, until the intuitive recognition of the material was complete and resounding. As such this process offered me a valuable educational trajectory in my creative development and nurtured a strong 'felt' understanding of a new creative methodology.

> This compositional approach seems necessarily to be a risky one. The form such a piece will take can rarely be predicted at the outset and clarity does not always ensue. Sometimes the sheer complexity of thought renders it resistant to physicalization, and it remains subdued, mute, not flowing through the body, or through the form of the dance. However, when it does happen that thought and feeling and movement are fully integrated, each embodied in the other, then a truly eloquent work may be created. [Dempster, 1985: 19]

Chamber was a complex work. The sheer weight of time and thought that collected around it gave it a very dense quality. Engaging with both physical and theoretical perspectives, and their points of intersection, created an ongoing tension in its inception and realization. There needed to be a mutual interaction between these two aspects, which ultimately gave the work much greater depth, but it was also a constant shackle. As I was attempting to work intuitively in the studio, the theoretical concerns took time to assimilate. While the intentions inherent in *Chamber* may at times be complicated as a consequence of this interaction, my belief is that the work is more mature and considered because of it.

Conclusion
This project began as a response to predominant attitudes toward dancing, but more particularly toward male dancing. These attitudes were reflective of the notion that men should treat the body with suspicion because of its association with femininity, so as not to disturb the seeming tranquillity surrounding the hegemonic projection of the idealized man. Within this dualistic image the body is denied and rejected, as are any practices which do not comply with the ideals of hegemonic masculinity Those practices which do not comply with this patriarchal dictate are identified by the dominant entity as feminine. But I, like so many men, feel at odds with this limited construction of masculine identity. The tranquillity that masculinity might present at first glance is not in fact easily sustainable. But because of its unquestioned prevalence, hegemonic masculinity is in need of scrutiny, particularly as the imbalance it necessitates is so destructive to both women and men.

The power patriarchy wields to expel has, to a large degree, cast out the embodied practice of dancing, substantially diminishing the acceptability of the practice. In a sense, patriarchy has been indiscriminate about gender in this instance, affecting both male and female dancers. Yet because it has overwhelmingly been women who are diminished by patriarchy (in all areas of life) it has been the central and unifying concern of the feminist movement to challenge its dominance. As a result of the myriad of voices who have emerged and have made such a significant impact with theoretical feminism, a great deal of thought and pressure has been applied to the issue. It is partially from within this body of knowledge, particularly the work of Grosz, that this project has sought to locate itself.

I too have drawn on the ideas of Maurice Merleau-Ponty because of the resistance he offers to dualistic notions of mind and body. His radical siting of the body as the seat of subjectivity also has implications for this project, by giving the body, and by implication dancing, validity and power. When Merleau-Ponty claims "The perceiving mind is an incarnated body" [Merleau-Ponty, 1964: 3], he could be speaking for dance practices which seek to draw on the experiences of the body and refute instrumental approaches to the body. His ideas also offer the possibility that the body is not merely or only a sign, but something that has a degree of autonomy from the symbolic order and can be a way of 'knowing' which operates on its own terms. Dance, then, is also a form of 'self-knowing' which strongly defines the practice as a form of embodied subjectivity.

Viewed from this perspective, in *Chamber*, a dance piece about masculine subjectivity, the act of men dancing can be seen in new light. The male dancers can be seen to be negotiating their subjectivity through their bodies. It is as men that they become associated with embodiment, and by so doing challenge the aversion hegemony has toward men being attentive to their bodies beyond the ritualised enactments of power and control.

The choreographic methodology for this focus has been to use improvisation both as a thought-provoking creative tool and as a performance medium. Improvisation has a phenomenological dimension which complements Merleau-Ponty's ideas regarding embodied subjectivity. It has also operated as a strategy to create a more open possibility for masculine identification and to resist the masculinist insistence on closure. As choreographer of *Chamber*, the traditional role has also been altered within this strategy. I no longer acted as the sole authority in the process but was necessarily open to the contributions and perspectives of the dancers. *Chamber* was a work specific to the experiences of the men involved. It did not aim to make universal claims for all men, but only to detail the experiences of the three men and of myself as choreographer.

Indeed, the making and performance of *Chamber* was an intensely personal and challenging process for all involved. As a structured improvisation it placed quite specific demands on the dancers. Each dancer was continually being asked to re-find or to re-invent dance material. This was from a perspective that required a sensitive 'listening' to their own kinaesthetic, emotional and intellectual responses to a movement score or the structure of the piece as a whole. The resulting performances have an integrity and force behind them because of the investment made by all artists involved. If the anecdotal reactions to the performances by audiences can be accepted then *Chamber* made an impact. This impact might be small in the larger scheme of things, but significant in its political stance and a thoughtful (but possibly unexpected) contribution to the debates about masculinity. I hope that seeing male dancers struggle with these problems in a physical form can offer an example for other men and challenge them to think how hegemony can distort and impoverish the range of possibilities for men. I also hope that *Chamber* can elicit for men some new sense of their bodies as profound and affective entities. Finally, I hope that this can in some small way diffuse the distrust and misunderstanding many men feel for the rich and multifaceted form that is dance.

BIBLIOGRAPHY

Albright, A. C. (1997). *Choreographing Difference. The Body and Identity in Contemporary Dance*. Hanover, Wesleyan University Press.

Banes, S. (1980). *Terpsichore in Sneakers. Post-Modern Dance*. Boston, Houghton Mifflin.

Baxter, J. K. (1982). 'The Black Star' in J. E. Weir (ed.) *Selected Poems. James K. Baxter*. Auckland, Oxford University Press.

Belgrad, D. (1998). *The Culture of Spontaneity: Improvisation and the Arts in Postwar America*. Chicago, University of Chicago Press.

Bhaba, H. K. (1995). 'Are You a Man or a Mouse?' in B. Wallis, S. Watson and M. Berger *Constructing Masculinity*. New York, Routledge.

Bigwood, C. (1998). 'Renaturalizing the Body (with the Help of Merleau-Ponty)' in D. Welton (ed.) *Body and Flesh. A Philosophical Reader*. Massachusetts, Blackwell.

Bordo, S. (1994). 'Reading the Male Body' in L. Goldstein (ed.) *The Male Body. Features, Destinies, Exposures*. Ann Arbor, University of Michigan Press.

_____, (1998). 'Bringing Body to Theory' in D. Welton (ed.) *Body and Flesh. A Philosophical Reader*. Malden, Massachusetts, Blackwell.

_____, (1998). '"Material Girl": The Effacements of Postmodern Culture' in D. Welton (ed.) *Body and Flesh. A Philosophical Reader*. D. Welton. Malden, Massachusetts, Blackwell.

Buchholz, E. L. (1999). *Goya*. Cologne, Konemann Verlagsgesellschaft mbH.

Burt, R. (1995). *The Male Dancer. Bodies, Spectacle, Sexualities*. London, Routledge.

Butler, J. (1990). 'Performative Acts and Gender Constitution: An Essay in Phenomenology and Feminist Theory' in S. E. Case (ed.) *Performing Feminisms: Feminist Critical theory and Theatre*. Baltimore, John Hopkins University Press.

_____, (1998). Selections from Bodies that Matter in D. Welton (ed.) *Body and Flesh. A Philosophical Reader*. Malden, Massachusetts, Blackwell.

Butterworth, J. (1998). Lloyd Newson interviewed by Jo Butterworth. *Dance Makers Portfolio. Conversations with Choreographers*. J. Butterworth & G. Clarke, The Centre for Dance and Theatre Studies, University of Bretton.

Christian, H. (1994). *The Making of Anti-sexist men.* London, Routledge.

Connell, R. W. (1987). *Gender and Power.* Sydney, Allen and Unwin.

_____, (1995). *Masculinities.* St Leonards, NSW, Allen and Unwin.

_____, (2000). *The Men and the Boys*. Sydney, Allen & Unwin.

Cranny-Francis, A. (1995). *The Body in the Text*. Melbourne, Melbourne University Press

De Spain, K. (1993). "Dance Improvisation: Creating Chaos" in *Contact Quarterly*, (Vol. 18, No. 1): 21-27.

_____, (1995). "A Moving Decision. Notes on the Improvising Mind," in *Contact Quarterly*, (Vol. 20, No. 1): 48-50.

Dempster, E. (1985). "Imagery, ideokinesis and choreography," in *Writings on Dance* (1): 18-22.

Fausto-Sterling, A. (1995). 'How to Build a Man' in *Constructing Masculinity*. M. Berger, B. Wallis & S. Watson. New York, Routledge.

Fensham, R. (1993). "Dancing in and out of Language. A Feminist Dilemma," in *Writings on Dance* (9): 22-39.

Foster, S. L. (1986). *Reading Dancing. Bodies and Subjects in Contemporary American Dance*. Berkeley, University of California Press.

_____, (1996). 'The Ballerina's Phallic Pointe' in S. L. Foster (ed.) *Corporealities: Dancing knowledge, Culture and Power*. London, Routledge.

Fraleigh, S. H. (1987). *Dance and the Lived body. A Descriptive Aesthetics*. Pittsburgh, University of Pittsburgh Press.

Gardner, S. (1996). "Spirit of Gravity and maiden's feet," in *Writings on Dance* (15): 48-61.

Garner, S. B. (1994). *Bodied Spaces. Phenomenology and Performance in Contemporary Drama*. New York, Cornell University Press.

Goldstein, L., Ed. (1994). *The Male Body. Features, Destinies, Exposures*. Ann Arbor, University of Michigan Press.

Grosz, E. (1994).*Volatile Bodies. Toward a Corporeal Feminism*. St Leonards, NSW, Allen & Unwin.

_____, (1999). *Merleau-Ponty and Irigaray in the Flesh. Merleau-Ponty, Interiority and Exteriority, Psychic Life and the World*. D. Olkowski & J. Morley. Albany, State University of New York.

Heckes, F. (1998). *Reason and Folly. The Prints of Francisco Goya*. National Gallery of Victoria, Melbourne

Hekman, S. (1998). 'Material Bodies' in D. Welton (ed.) *Body and Flesh. A Philosophical Reader*. Malden, Massachusetts, Blackwell.

Langer, M. M. (1989). *Merleau-Ponty's Phenomenology of Perception. A Guide and Commentary*. Tallahassee, Florida State University Press.

Lori b, S. P. (1996). "The Sex Issue. Lori b and Steve Paxton interview each other," in *Contact Quarterly* (Winter/Spring): 43-51.

Luckhurst, M. (1997). DV8... Ten Years on the Edge, DV8 Physical Theatre. Available: <http//: www.dv8.co.uk> (June 2002)

Mansfield, N. (2000). *Subjectivity. Theories of the Self from Freud to Harraway*. New York, New York University Press.

Martin, R. (1990). *Performance as Political Act. The Embodied Self*. New York, Bergin and Garvey.

Merleau-Ponty, M. (1962). *Phenomenology of Perception*. London, Routledge & Kegan Paul.

_____, (1964). *The Primacy of Perception*. Evanston, Northwestern University Press.

Middleton, P. (1992). *The Inward Gaze. Masculinity and Subjectivity in Modern Culture*. London, Routledge.

Novack, C. J. (1990). *Sharing the Dance. Contact Improvisation and American Culture.* Madison, Wisconsin, The University of Wisconsin Press.

Paxton, S. (1977). "In the midst of standing still something else occurs and the name for that is the small dance," in *Theatre Papers* (Series 1, no 4).

_____, (1992). Improvisation is... *Contact Quarterly's Contact Improvisation Sourcebook.* Northampton, Massachusetts, Contact editions: 125-129.

Priest, S. (1998). *Merleau-Ponty.* London, Routledge.

Robinson, V. (1996). 'Heterosexuality and masculinity: theorising male power or the wounded male psyche?' in D. Richardson (ed.) *Theorising Heterosexuality. Telling it Straight.* Buckingham, Open University Press.

Rothfield, P. (1994/5). "Philosophies of Movement," in *Writings on Dance* (11/12): 77-86.

Rutherford, J. (1988). 'Who's that Man?' in R. Chapman & J. Rutherford (eds) *Male Order: Unwrapping Masculinity.* London, Lawrence and Wishart.

_____, (1992). *Men's Silences. Predicaments in Masculinity.* London, Routledge.

Ryan, T. (1985). 'Roots of Masculinity' in A. Metcalf and M. Humphries (eds) *The Sexuality of Men.* London, Pluto Press.

Seidler, V. J. (1989). *Rediscovering Masculinity. Reason, Language and Sexuality.* London, Routledge.

_____, (1997). *Man Enough. Embodying Masculinities.* London, Sage.

States, B. O. (1992). 'The Phenomenological Attitude' in J. G. Reinelt. & J. R. Roach (eds) *Critical Theory and Performance.* Ann Arbor, The University of Michigan Press.

Suleiman, S. R., Ed. (1985). *The Female Body in Western Culture. Contemporary Perspectives.* Cambridge, Massachusetts, Harvard University Press.

Todd, M. E. (1937). *The Thinking Body.* Princeton, NJ, Princeton Book Company.

Tushingham, D. (1995). Lloyd Newson... Dance About Something, DV8 Physical Theatre. Available: <http//: www.dv8.co.uk> (June 2002)

Williams, D. (1996). "Working (In) the In-between. Contact Improvisation as an Ethical Practice." *Writings on Dance* (15): 23-37.

Young, I. (1998). 'Throwing like a Girl' in D. Welton *Body and Flesh. A Philosophical Reader.* Malden, Massachusetts, Blackwell.

CHAMBER
masculinity, identity & improvisation

> *...finally after much deliberation he entered. It was an ambiguous, slippery interior where what he believed to be solid began to crumble; where what he thought was his began to seem ill-fitting; and where what he had never imagined began to emerge from the shadows of the darkened room...*

Direction/concept: Shaun McLeod
Performance: Simon Ellis, Martin Kwasner, Jacob Lehrer
Sound: David Corbet
Video: Cormac Lally & Christina Shepard
Lighting Design: Matt Delbridge
Voice-Overs: Ben Grant
Text: James K Baxter, Readers Digest Complete Book of the Garden (1973)

This project would not have been possible without the support and tremendous goodwill of everybody involved. A huge thank you to all the artists for their inspiring contributions. Cobie Orger has also been invaluable as publicity liaison person. I would also like to thank Kim Vincs, Tim Davey, Suzanne Hurley, Kath Papas, Mitch Buzza, Heather Ruck, Tim Harvey and Digitools.

This project has been supported by Deakin University and the University of Melbourne.

Biographies

Shaun McLeod has danced with Australian Dance Theatre, One Extra and Danceworks. As choreographer he has made work for ADT, Danceworks, VCA and Deakin University as well as producing his own performances. He also loves dance improvisation having performed as a solo artist and with the improvisational collective Catch Cry who produced *Fallow* for Danceworks. He is particularly interested in the integration of improvisational methods with structured choreography. He currently teaches dance at Deakin University.

Simon Ellis is an independent dancer, choreographer and teacher. His work is influenced by dance and theatre traditions, and also by visual design. Simon has worked with Big Fish Dance, Shona McCullagh, Michael Parmenter, Don Asker, Shaun McLeod and Anna Smith. His own work includes *Touch* (1998), *Semi-detached* (1999), and *undone years* (2000). Simon is currently preparing to spend four months in the United States working on a dance video project, and in early 2002 he will perform for the Douglas Wright Dance Company.

Jacob Lehrer has a mixed bag of experience. From the highs of the International Outdoor Festival circuit (with Strange Fruit) to the depths of the black box we call the Theatre (with the likes of Lloyd Newson's DV8 Physical Theatre). A practitioner of Contact Improvisation (with State of Flux) Jacob has been enjoying working with these fellows and others in Melbourne.

Martin Kwasner is a graduate of the VCA. He has worked with various dance and theatre companies including 2 Dance Plus, Didi Koi Dance, Danceworks, Big Fish, Dance Compass Melbourne and Handspan Visual Theatre. He also has considerable experience as an independent artist and choreographer. He is currently developing a solo work to be performed at the Asian Contemporary Dance Festival in Osaka, Japan.

David Corbet David Corbet studied in a Bachelor of Music and a Bachelor of Arts at Melbourne Uni. Since then he has composed music across a wide range of genres including much music for dance and theatre. Recent collaborations include works with Ros Crisp and Jonathon Sinatra.

Christina Shepard comes to film from a dance background having performed with Meryl Tankard in Canberra and Tasdance. Since entering the film world she has worked mainly as a freelance editor on projects including a feature film and the SBS 5 part documentary series *Once Were Monks*. Christina is currently completing a professional writing course.

Cormac Lally is a freelance editor and camera operator working for various production companies Melbourne including Digitools. He also works with visual artists, such as David Rozetsky, as editor/technical supervisor having been involved with exhibitions in Australia, New Zealand and Europe. Cormac worked on the upcoming documentary *Black Cat, Night Cat*.

Printed in the United Kingdom
by Lightning Source UK Ltd.
136280UK00001B/148/P